The Modern Witch's Spellbook

The Modern Witch's Spellbook

Everything You Need to Know to Cast Spells,
Work Charms and Love Magic, and
Achieve What You Want in Life
Through Occult Powers

by Sarah Lyddon Morrison

THE CITADEL PRESS   Secaucus, New Jersey

THE MODERN WITCH'S SPELLBOOK

ISBN 0-8065-0372-6

ACKNOWLEDGMENT

My thanks to David St. Clair for permission to use his tale of Brazilian
magic; it also appears in his new book, *Drum and Candle*, published by
Doubleday and Company, Inc.

Published by Citadel Press
A division of Lyle Stuart Inc.
120 Enterprise Avenue, Secaucus, N.J. 07094
In Canada: Musson Book Company
A division of General Publishing Co. Limited
Don Mills, Ontario
Manufactured in the United States of America

For my dear, long-suffering husband, Ralph,
who lives with the constant fear that he's been bewitched

Contents

The Modern Witch's Spellbook

Introduction

$\mathcal{P}$ersonally, I find the whole idea of sacrificing chickens and crucifying toads upside down abysmal. The very thought of sipping warm, fresh goat's blood from a chalice makes my tongue quiver. Squeamish and city-bred, I, and many others, I suspect, could not deal with these and other important rituals in a true black witchcraft ceremony. I'm not so sure that many people could handle midnight coven meetings in remote cemeteries, or a vision of the sabbatic goat rising from a flaming altar, either.

If you're into black magic, you're a very brave, inured person, and, some psychiatrists say, psychotic. In cultures where black ceremonies are part of everyday religious ritual it's perfectly normal to deal with devils and conjure evil spirits; in our own Western culture, however, only the off-beat dare to call up the evil Lucifer, knowing that devils here are not only widely frowned on, but thought to be real only by persons with a psychopathic imagination.

Fortunately for Westerners intrigued by magic and wishing to indulge in it, the black arts are only one area of sorcery—albeit a large and important one. There is also white magic, which, with almost the same techniques as black, is used to achieve edifying rather than evil ends. There are also gypsy and other folk magic, objects that have magical properties (such as amulets and talismans), in fact a whole area of spells and charms that might be lumped under the term informal magic. The laborious process of formal magic, black and white, requires the use of pentacles, consecrated wands, and, sometimes, nudity in the company of other witches. But the equally effective informal magic requires only a few easily obtainable items: herbs, wax, etc.—and a willing heart.

Practitioners of formal magic scorn us modern, less classic witches (a phrase I use to mean, roughly, sorcerers—not followers of the witchcraft religion) with our nonviolent ceremonies and civilized hearts. They consider us benign dabblers in something we know nothing about. And, because of our ignorance, accidental creators of mischief. They say that a non-classic witch fooling around with spells is like a layman fooling around with live electric wires. We're not dabblers, and we're definitely not benign; but on the accidental mischief point, classic magicians are right, to an extent.

When I cast my first spell on someone it backfired. I worked in an office with a particularly annoying individual, and I thought I'd bewitch him so he'd leave and take a job elsewhere. Within a few days everyone in my office *except* the person I was after contracted what came to be known as "leaving fever." During the next month, all but a handful of the original staff left for other jobs. Except, of course, the person I'd bewitched.

Some time later I came across a practicing sorcerer and told him about my experiences. He said, "Oh, you have to expect that. The first half-dozen spells I cast backfired with some startling results, too, but after a while you figure out what you've been doing wrong and things start going the way you plan." My only feeling on backfires is that if a novice modern witch undertakes a spell, she must be wise enough to know that it's a time-tested recipe, and any deviation from it can cause a mess she'll wish she didn't have to put her name to. Just be very careful—that's all any beginner can do.

No matter how complex or simple the ritual, the force that makes a magic spell work is the same in all cases. Nine days of fasting, little sleep, and the intoxicating fumes of narcotic herbs burning on an altar may produce a devil to do your bidding, but overwhelming emotion conjured in a few minutes of concentrated hatred, love, or avarice can also create desired results. For the power of magic is in the force of an emotion directed at a person or object.

The key, of course, is that not just any old emotion will do. There are degrees of feeling, and in magic, only the highest pitch of emotion has any effect whatsoever. Part of being a witch, classic or not, is developing an ability to arouse an enormous quantity of feeling, and it takes superhuman concentration to summon and project it properly. It's also perfectly useless to aspire to become a witch without the ability to form clear mental images in the mind's eye. Many people, regrettably, don't think in pictures, but rather in words, and so are unable to create a photograph-perfect image of the person they wish to bewitch. It's essential to be able to focus mentally on the subject while at the same time casting powerful thought-waves of emotion at him.

What magicians do, really, is to will waves of hatred or love at a person by telepathy, for lack of a better word. More and more is being learned about the effects of strongly projected feelings—notably on plants, which react perceptibly to both human love and human hatred. Science fiction tells us that eventually we will be able to communicate telepathically with each other, perhaps even to freeze an enemy in his tracks with a look. Magic, mankind's oldest religion, has always celebrated the power of the mind to control and alter relationships. Perhaps the concept of ancient magic will in the future govern every aspect of our lives.

The Sumerians, Babylonians, Assyrians, Egyptians, Hebrews, Greeks, and Romans embraced and passed along the magical traditions that eventually emerged in Europe as sorcery. Witchcraft, a full-blown religion of some influence from about 1450 to 1750, grew out of sorcery but developed separate beliefs. Witches, meeting in covens at Sabbats, conjured Satan, worshipped him, and contracted with him for the power to work evil magic. As payment, they publicly scorned God and Christianity. Traditional sorcerers, however, did not malign God; instead, conjuring the lords of the universe until they responded to the incantations and appeared, they sought, with God's blessing, to capture them and use their powers to control the universe.

All the good and evil facets of a man (love and hate, generosity and avarice, godliness and lust), a classical sorcerer believed, were to be found represented in the lords of the cosmos (for example, human greed is embodied in a god of avarice). A sorcerer attempted, by a process of mind expansion, to reach out and encompass these god-powers, to subject them to his will. In black ceremonies, for example, a magician, after calling on God to protect him physically from the devils he wished to conjure, worked himself into a trance, perhaps burning narcotic herbs to facilitate the process. Then, when his mind was free of his body (Indians call this state *satori*), he let it grow, finally encompassing the powers of the god he'd conjured. He became that god. He then called on the great spirit he'd become—perhaps Lucifer, Bealzebuth, or Asteroth—to do his bidding, commanding him (in his omnipotent, free-mind state) to kill an enemy, or lead him to a cache of buried treasure.

To help him achieve the power of a god, the sorcerer, like

Faust, sought knowledge and more knowledge; like the Renaissance man, he aspired to be complete, a master of all things. In the tradition of King Solomon, an all-time master magician, he prayed to Jehovah for protection and help in his undertakings, and, if following the instructions of a European *grimoire* (magical textbook), he might sequester himself for as long as six months to meditate, study holy books, and prepare himself for his magical feat. He fasted, abstained from sex, went through endless, self-disciplined hours of prayer ritual, made magical implements, consecrated everything he made as a priest might, and stitched mystical symbols on his silken robes.

Behind the glass façades of New York apartment buildings and the walls of sumptuous European villas and townhouses, there are sorcerers today who are spending a lifetime diligently pursuing magical works.

Covens of contemporary witches with traditional beliefs, in surprising numbers (there are about four hundred covens in the United States), also spend considerable time strolling down the left-hand path. The popularity of classical witchcraft, with its worship of the devil, proliferates among the young and the disaffected.

Some psychologists say that people turn to magic in time of great uncertainty, when the importance of the individual seems to slip away and life becomes cheap. Biblical Jews turned to Moses, who was regarded as a powerful sorcerer, to save them from the fearsome Egyptians, and it is entirely possible that Christianity flourished because people came to believe that the protective magic of Jesus (perhaps the world's greatest magician) was stronger than that of other magicians, Hebrew and Roman. I'm simply speculating, of course, but Jesus, according to the Bible, was adept at such magical operations as raising the dead and, with the touch of a hand, healing the sick. It is also true that we live in an age of superbombs with a behemoth government whose intentions are not always clear to the public; the appeal of magic steadily increases.

There are many varieties of magic—for example, the religions such as witchcraft and voodoo, or folk magic with its potions and spells. What they offer in common to practitioners is power—the power to destroy enemies, to stir love, to become rich, to control fate. There are numberless occasions in a lifetime when a magical charm or spell can be useful; at such moments, it is comforting to know that by the use of magic the course of events has been, as much as possible, favorably directed.

The magical methods an individual chooses are entirely a matter of personal taste. I find hard-core, classical witchcraft unappetizing, classical sorcery a time-consuming, complicated muddle (formal magic, as explained in the few authentic grimoires that exist, is impossible to attain without the aid of a magical scholar sitting at your elbow). Voodoo just isn't in my blood. But the magical spells and amulets (most of them rooted in classical sorcery) as employed by village witches and gypsies in Europe, by the peasant girls of many countries, and, in some cases, the early Hebrews and Egyptians, have a certain sanity, even charm (in the instance of certain love spells), that appeals to my modern sensibilities. I find that if a ceremony is truly outrageous to me, really turns me off, there's no sense in trying to see it through: I don't concentrate on the subject of the spell then, but dwell on the repulsiveness of the ceremony. Without complete concentration on the subject of the ceremony, no spell can work. And spells can and do work.

This book contains magical operations that, as much as possible, are in accord with contemporary proprieties (meaning I've avoided ceremonies that call for animal sacrifices, for example). This is a "how-to" guide for modern witches, a collection of recipes that, if carefully cooked up, can have powerful results. It is always wise, when using unfamiliar ingredients, to start with simple recipes. I have included some of these, as well as one or two highly complex ceremonies. I have also included a list of shops in New York where you may write to buy some of the more esoteric herbs (it's possible to purchase a whole mandrake root) that are occasionally called for.

There are a number of qualities that a modern witch should possess if she hopes to be successful in her craft. Her mind must be "pictorial" (able to think in pictures) and, certainly, highly disciplined. She should also have an open mind (one that's inquiring enough to seek new ideas). And she must have courage. Wondering what's inside Pandora's box is not the same as opening it and finding out; a witch must be able to face down fear. If you're all-together in these areas, you will probably do well as a witch.

Part I

LOVE MAGIC

CHAPTER I

Charms and Spells

Since Adam first swore at Eve for giving him that ridiculous piece of fruit from the Tree of Knowledge and getting them both thrown out of Paradise, true love has run a bumpy course pitted with frustrations. Even the powerful gods of Olympus, with all their hereditary magical talents, were rendered impotent to direct smooth and happy love affairs of their own: the goddess Hera was helplessly reduced to transforming her husband's mistresses into cows and other unattractive beasts.

King Solomon, with magical powers that made him as immortal as a mortal can be, was once heard to remark anxiously, "I have a thousand wives and none of them are any good." He never did discover the secret incantation that would find him the perfect mate. Ah, frustration!

Not until the reign of Louis XIV was solid progress of any kind made toward finding the solution to unhappy love and marriage situations. Then, Louis's courtiers and other royal sycophants took to poisoning unwanted wives and husbands. This technique, however, caused a scandal that brought fortune-tellers, counts, and countesses in an endless stream to the Star Chamber for a national accounting. It was even revealed that the royal mistress, Madame de Montespan, had plans to poison the king! So the practice was dropped as a poor idea.

Never mind. In the villages of Europe, over the centuries, the bright, practical peasants quietly accumulated a vast storehouse of working charms and spells that do exactly what they are supposed to do: resolve the frustrations and miseries of love. Out there in the country, generations of French and Italian girls, Rumanian and gypsy maids have been successfully snagging devious, fleet-footed lovers—by bewitchment—and bringing them to heel and the altar. And we're still fumbling around relying completely on our overworked wits!

The time has come to take ourselves in hand and pay some heed to the folk witches' magic. They've used the same formulas for hundreds of years, and if the spells weren't efficacious, they wouldn't have survived. Mothers wouldn't have bothered daughters to carefully memorize charms that were useless; and daughters wouldn't have made *their* offspring agonize over recipes for love spells that didn't work. In fact, virile young bloods wouldn't have taken up precious, secret hours to concoct—with bits of earth, parchment, and candles—love traps for their ladies if these traps never caught anybody. Local stregas, like African medicine men, would long since have been out of jobs if their decoctions never stirred a heart to love. Doesn't it seem peculiar that we haven't learned *something* from them?

But in our glass-wrapped skyscraper cities, we're faced with up-to-date concerns such as air pollution, overcrowding, and poverty, and our minds have been reduced, lately, to near-brainless sounding boards reverberating with the deafening noise of rock music, TV commercials, Cape Kennedy, and politicians endlessly haranguing us about war and riots. When we actually stop to think of so remote a subject as magic, we tend to perceive it in terms of future scientific marvels—finding fuels to make spaceships travel at the speed of light, or a way to dematerialize our bodies on earth and rematerialize them, seconds later, on a distant star light-years away. Our magical feats seem far removed indeed from the medieval sorcerer's.

But there is a continuity between the magical works of the past and the future. Both magician and scientist seek a similar goal: to vanquish and control nature, and even the mind and body of man. Suspend our disbelief in the efficacy of traditional magic, and we can use it as we would a modern consciousness-expanding drug. The trick is to explore the powers of the mind—to control and strongly focus them, and then attain seemingly impossible goals with them.

One of the most difficult accomplishments, it would appear, is to move a recalcitrant, perhaps uninterested, heart to love. And yet it's easy to do if the proper strong emotion is conjured, focused with great concentration through a potent spell, and leveled like a bolt of lightning at the person desired. It takes practice to make magic work, and an expenditure of time and effort; like anything else, there can be no stinting if there is to be success.

One of the basic concepts of magic—black or white, formal or informal—is that nothing that occurs in the universe is a random event. This principle derives from classical sorcery's concept of the cosmos as being something like a giant puzzle, with each piece necessary, each, in its place, affecting all the others. One hand (that of God) puts them all together in a pattern. (This concept, incidentally, is the basis for astrology.) When an event takes place now, it can be used to help predict future events, for all parts of the universe puzzle relate.

Heavenly happenings also have their influence on earthly life, and as events occur on earth, they affect events that are taking place in the rarified realms of heaven (it's a *universe* puzzle, not an earth one). This happens, naturally, because both planes are controlled by one player's hand, God's.

If the traditional sorcerer wished to manipulate events on earth, he had only to call on their heavenly counterpart powers to change them. Lust, hate, famine, plague, what-have-you are embodied in the forms of dozens of different devils, each with assigned spheres of influence. To material-ize the correct devil, the sorcerer conjured it in a specially designed magical ceremony until the devil appeared.

Conjuring a force, of course, was useless unless one in-tended to have it to do something specific. If the devil was supposed to harm someone, or, in a lighter vein, inspire love, then a physical connection with the victim had to be estab-lished so that the devil would know whom you were talking about. The connection, as it turns out, could be a bit of the subject's hair, or something from a well-worn garment, even a toenail clipping. (Rather like giving a bloodhound a sniff of an escaped convict's shirt before sending him in pursuit.) In fact a connection could be established by simply saying, over some wax, or parchment, "this represents such and such a person."

The concept of the physical connection in magic has found its way into many folk love charms. You must be pre-pared to spend some time plotting ways to get hold of such items as hair or an old shoe belonging to a prospective lover.

◄§ *To Catch a Man* §►

An excellent love charm for a beginning witch to try her hand at—because it exercises the powers of concentration, and requires the mind to focus, over a period of time, on the intended victim—is also a fairly simple one to make. And it demonstrates the use of symbolic magical connections.

Take some earth from the footprint of the man you love. (More easily done by country or beach witches, this feat requires ingenuity in the city. Perhaps you can catch him in a park, or arrange to drop a flower pot of dirt just where he is about to step, to catch his print.) Put the earth in a pot, and plant a sunflower in it. As the sunflower flourishes, your man's love for you will blossom.

The dirt from the footprint is, obviously, the symbolic connection with *him*, and an essential ingredient. Sunflowers are a magical flower, well-known in Europe and America for their powers. Summer brides carry them in wedding bouquets, and herbalists use them. Because the flower follows the sun, it absorbs its energy and potency.

Remember that it's important to apply a strong measure of emotion whenever you tend the plant; visualize your man in detail and forcefully project desire at his image. Do this often, but only when you are rested; you must be able to expend considerable emotional energy without straining your resources during the vital moments of concentration. A minute or two should be sufficient time for this ceremony on any given occasion, but continue the concentration if you have the slightest feeling that the quality of your projection isn't up to par.

It does seem, sometimes, as if the ingredients found in magical charms were chosen by the same diabolical brains that invented such pastimes as treasure hunts and practical jokes. It must be remembered, however, that magic has its roots deep in the country lives of pastoral peoples; while trees may be difficult for city dwellers to come by, they're as easy to find as grass for country people. So it should come as no surprise that in peasant charms, especially, natural ingredients were most popular. Living close to the land as they did, peasants leaned heavily to trees, swiftly running streams, herbs, and fresh eggs for charms; serious, modern city witches using such spells are just going to have to face the fact that occasional sorties to the country are necessary.

Unless you're the proud owner of a garden or landscaped terrace, there seems to be little hope of your coming across a willow tree in the city. Such a tree is required in the following English spell to catch a husband (incidentally, this one is also recommended for beginners).

Stalk your lover, and when you can, secretly remove the earth from his footprint. Take it to a willow tree and carefully bury it near the trunk. While doing this, mutter the following incantation with the requisite feeling, concentration, and projection:

> Green grass and willow tree
> His captured soul I bring to thee,
> Grow his love, grow for me
> As green grows the willow tree.

A more sophisticated English love spell of the footprint ilk (this sort of magic was used by almost all Europeans) requires that you actually know the young man you're after to the degree that he would incuriously accept a little edible goodie from you without suspecting your ulterior motives.

Take some earth from his footprint, and some of your own nail clippings. Mix both ingredients with essence of orange and arrange that he eat them.

There are no special directions for serving this diabolical powder to your lover, so you can use some initiative here. My feeling is that Betty Crocker spice cake could make a fine disguise, because the spices speckle the cake, anyway, and a few extra speckles will go unnoticed. Brownies cooked with pot were happily made in a movie, and they can also be used here to hide your dirty work. Whatever morsel you choose to present him with, your thoughtfulness will be rewarded.

Men are always saying that the way to their hearts is through their stomachs—but they probably wouldn't grin so complacently if they knew about two fine old gypsy love charms that work on a similar theory. In fact, they wouldn't speak to lady witches again if they thought for a moment that such spells were even being *considered* for use on them. They're frightening.

These two love charms are not for the delicate, or for unpracticed witches—they're strictly for unshockable, sophisticated free souls. We're getting into black magic here— or at the edges of it, anyway—and so you should understand some more magical theory.

There's nothing so powerful in magic as a connection to a victim made with something from your own body. Through such a connection, you're laying overwhelming will, your magic force, directly on a person, and he must at once fall under your spell. Here's how the gypsy girls do it:

Collect in a field, at night, some fresh mushrooms. Take them home, mince them, and mix with two drops of your blood. (You can prick your finger with a needle.) Serve the concoction to your intended lover with his mashed potatoes.

The other potion is easier to make, as you don't need to find a field and go groping around in the night for mushrooms.

Let some blood fall upon one of your used handkerchiefs (sorry, paper ones won't do) and let it dry. Now burn the hanky and scatter the ash in his salad. (Naturally, with both charms, you apply appropriate witchly concentration.)

Should that attractive man turn out to be a satyr or something equally annoying, you can turn off his interest by capturing some personal item from him (a sock?) and burning it.

Modern witches have certain advantages over their medieval sisters because magic is not now widely studied or understood; few people, therefore, are really aware of what's going on when they're being bewitched. Who among us could accurately fathom the intention of a smiling apple-cheeked girl who (in pursuit of magic spell ingredients) kindly whisks away a precariously dangling lash from the corner of her lover's eye ("There, you almost had an eye-winker"), or requests a snippet of her man's Cardin suit ("The color is gorgeous, and I want a dress made up in it—you won't miss a tiny bit from the lining")? Hair is easy to come by ("I've always thought you'd look great in an Afro. Let me comb it up and see"), although nail parings can be tricky ("Ouch, your fingernails scratched me—just let me trim them for you"). If he bites his nails, you're out of luck.

But even trickier to bring off, unless you're lucky enough to be an *au pair* girl with access to his closet, the board chairman's secretary, or a crafty topless waitress, is what's required in the following charm to capture a man:

Steal his necktie. Wear it about your waist.

Fortunately, witches don't have to spend all their time engaged in petty larceny. It's sometimes possible to *give* a man his fateful dose of magic. And quite pleasantly, too. You can be relaxed and in a confident frame of mind, because *no one* is suspicious of gifts any more. (It was different in the old days. Remember, "Beware of Greeks bearing gifts"?) Here's how to charm and snare him:

Find a triple-yolked egg. Give it to him, fried. He'll find you irresistible.

You probably can work this charm most unobtrusively at breakfast-time, or midnight suppers only, unless you can be counted on to do weird things like hand out triple-yolked fried eggs to men at any hour of the day or evening.

Since the beginning of time, women have tried *everything* to catch men. Southern girls wear hen feathers somewhere about their persons to attract love, and I know of a girl in Arizona who keeps a rattlesnake around as a little pet for the same purpose. Except for these and, really, amazingly few other wild exceptions, women have methodically trapped male affection with crafty, practical plots and snares.

In truth, catching a man is the high art of the female sex—an art whose techniques are carefully passed from mother to daughter through the generations. Men may ignore wallflowers, but women openly scorn them. Wallflower-ism represents female failure; no woman likes to see the red-rimmed eyes of the living proof that her own failure to lure a man is possible. To be proficiently guileful in a male world bent on staying bachelor is a girl's best hope. (Here, let us applaud the Women's Liberation Movement that would do away with this ridiculous bachelor-as-king syndrome.)

The fine hand of female craftiness can be detected in the mountains of aphrodisiacal recipes that proliferate in all parts of the world. Ancient Roman socialites served truffles, mushrooms, and peppers at their orgies, and Arab wives still take the fruits of the date palm, mash them well, and add them to olive oil for their husbands' breakfast eye-openers. And it's no peculiar racial quirk that prods Arabic beauties to slather themselves with the magnetic scent of musk, either.

On another, and seemingly less practical, level are magical love spells. These are, indeed, impractical if misunderstood; well used, however, they are the strongest weapon in woman's armory. Consider the ingredients in the next love

spell, of English origin. Rose petals attract love. The moon is
Venus' realm. A flower garden is a place of abundance, of
happiness. Taken together, they are powerfully symbolic,
and you can focus your telepathic force through them:

Go for a walk, naked, in the light of the moon, in a
flower garden, and cast behind you as you go handfuls
of rose petals. You will attract the lover you want.

Naturally, full concentration on a photograph-perfect
image of the desired lover is absolutely imperative while
performing this ceremony.

What are the odds, do you suppose, that you'll marry a
rich man? Every woman dreams up her own private utopia
(seldom middle-class and modestly appointed), but how
many airy palazzos with damask walls and gilded furniture,
marbled halls, and polished mirrors ever get built on solid
foundations?

Many more than you might think. Oh, the number of
legendary, super-rich women like Jackie Onassis is still
small, but it always will be. There are only one or two female scions counted at the top of the money heap in every
generation—though the wealth they need to be queen of this
mountain constantly escalates.

It's the ordinary souls who have country houses and city
apartments and vacation condominiums in the islands whose
numbers are, surprisingly, legion and ever growing. Their
husbands are the ones who started the grocery store down
the street—and now own fifty. Or the men who opened a
hotdog stand—and now own franchises on seven hundred of
them across the country. The odds of marrying a rich man
are better than ever, and your dreams of palaces have every
possibility of coming true.

What this next love charm does is help increase the odds.

But first, you must choose a likely man—one whose brains are in order, and whose neuroses aren't self-destructive. Then, to snare him, invite him to dinner. But first:

Make a stew of beef and lamb, and season it with marjoram and rosemary. Put in three or four cloves of garlic (to keep away the Evil Eye) and a large pinch of salt (to keep off all other evil influences). Now file your nails over the stew so that the dust from them falls in it, and pluck one or two hairs from all parts of your body and add them (these are your physical connections to him and will give you the upper hand). When the stew's done, serve it gleefully. He'll be helplessly drawn to you.

It is no surprise to me that researchers are making discoveries today that indicate that successful businessmen have greater ESP abilities than less successful ones. Many successful ones are consciously aware that they rely heavily on a sixth sense to make important business decisions. ESP works to help us in many areas of life. As one who is concerned with the unseen forces that often control us, I have had some experience with ESP myself, and not surprisingly, telepathy. They are the impulses behind all successful magical work.

Before my marriage, for example, if I wanted a certain man to call me for a date, I'd simply gather four or five of my friends together in a darkened room, light a candle, put it on the floor where we'd sit in a circle around it, and then, staring at it, concentrate on my man's name for four or five minutes. Everyone telepathized that this certain person should call me right away, and invariably he did. It worked for us all. After I had answered the phone, and made my date, I would return to the circle and we would concentrate for another girl in the group until she received *her* phone call. We did this perhaps once or twice a week. It *always* worked.

Don't sit around doubting the existence of telepathy— apply what I've just been talking about to this old American love spell:

When you see the man you're interested in, say his name over and over to yourself, backwards. Just before you go to sleep, wish hard to see him again (don't forget to visualize him). You will *definitely* see him again.

⟨§ To Keep Him ᙅ⟩

Girls just aren't taught properly when they're little to play their love cards close to their chests, and keep their hearts away from their sleeves. Little boys, on the other hand, somehow learn the tricks of the wily Arab horse trader, and grow up to use impassive eyes, set jaw muscles, and controlled emotions when dealing with women in matters of love. That's why it always appears that women are the pursuers of men and not vice versa. They aren't, really, but men are better equipped to make it seem that way. Male hearts palpitate when they fall in love, too—they just don't palpitate quite so openly as women's.

It's only natural, therefore, that when two people are in love, the woman is, usually, the one that's at a disadvantage. She's the lover with the anxieties like: "Will he call?" "What if he falls *out* of love with me suddenly?" She never stops to consider that her man may be just as anxious as she, because he *seems* so cool and unconcerned. He simply has the psychological edge on her.

So who needs that? Witches have always frowned on underdog situations, and their will to prevail is behind the following twentieth-century American spell to keep a man charmed in love.

Enter a church, and light a votive candle to the Virgin Mary. Then whisper:

> Dear Mother Mary, smile on me,
> Keep my love true to me,
> I want [speak his name]
> With all my heart
> And wish him never to depart.
> Dear Mother Mary, grant this me.

Yes, the difficulties of keeping a man, once you've got him, are increasing daily. With the social onus associated with divorce quickly dissipating, more of us are already involved in more honest alliances based on loving and caring for each other rather than on a sense of duty that requires us to stay married. When we stop loving and caring for each other, we simply get divorced. That is the trend.

Eventually, we will come to accept the fact that in our lifetimes we will probably have more than one mate. We live longer, we meet more people, we live at a faster, harder pace than any other humans ever have. We outgrow each other quickly as our interests multiply and insights into ourselves, our needs and aspirations, become clearer. If we marry in our early twenties, and divorce in our early thirties, it's often because we've grown up to be different people; marriage works best when there is continuing agreement in interests and outlook.

Ladies' magazines are always admonishing housewives who wish to keep their husbands intrigued to get busy and read, have hobbies, mix in community affairs, do *something* besides housework and raising the children. (This advice seems to reek like an old chestnut, as warnings just won't get you out of the house unless you're definitely motivated to do so.) Hausfrauism, nevertheless, is going out of style; it's not fashionable to be just a mommy anymore (and not financially practical for the mommy when divorce could strike at any moment and the alimony allowance possibly be modest).

So if you're a busy, involved, working mother full of up-to-date interests and ideas, with lots to talk about with your husband, you're *still* faced with keeping your relationship full of loving and caring! Here is a spell to keep your man in love with you:

> Take some of your own nail clippings and some of his, and burn them together at midnight (apply proper projection and concentration while doing the burning).

If your mind is expanded enough to be into witchcraft, you must also be aware enough to know that there are certain objects that you have owned (usually given to you) that had something rather unsavory about them. Perhaps it was a dress you bought, or that a man bought for you. Every time you wore it, something terrible happened. Maybe it was a ring. Every time you put it on, the day would end with you in tears over some matter. (I put this all in the past tense as I figure you had the good sense to rid yourself of the item long before this.)

There are, in fact, traditional gifts that bring you bad luck when they're given to you by a man. Keep this list handy, and if you are given something on it, check it out very carefully before you use or wear it. If there's the slightest hint that something's amiss with the item, give it away (to someone you don't like, it goes without saying).

> Rings of jade or turquoise.
> Bracelets of gold or silver set with pearls or garnets, amethysts, carnelians, opals, cat's-eyes, emeralds
> A locket (with his picture in it)

   Silver earrings, unless they are set with a lucky stone
   A peacock feather
   A leather box for jewelry
   A red handkerchief
   Walking shoes
   An oil portrait (of him)
   A mirror
   A parasol
   Windowshades
   A fingernail, a hair from his head
   A pair of ice tongs, a penknife
   A diary, pencil, quill pen

Any of the following trees and plants are bad luck for you:
anything scratchy, e.g., cactus, blackberry, nettle; roses,
poppy, dandelion; anything with an unpleasant odor, e.g.,
skunk cabbage, and all poisonous plants. Nut trees and dried
fruits bear watching.
   Watch out for these essences: jasmine, civet, carnation,
musk, lavender, ylang-ylang, all strong perfumes.

⤳§ To Get Him Back §⤵

Suppose you've aggressively gone about getting that attractive man to fall in love with you, and even seriously
entertain thoughts of marriage. You have a lovers' quarrel,
right? He raged unreasonably, didn't he, when he found out
the hard way you can't cook (my, but that fifteen-dollar filet
you destroyed looked peculiar!). Then your two afghans,
excited by the uproar, started leaping around and tore the
bells off his bell-bottoms, and he shouted "me or them" and
disappeared into the night!
   Ah, well. Get yourself together, and consider the possibilities. You're not about to give up your afghans, and you'll
probably never learn how to cook, so you can't really call

him and expect warm forgiveness—at least for a week. And he's supposed to take you skiing this weekend, and that's *tomorrow*. Don't panic.

Lovers have always faced absurd situations like this, and in the sixteenth century a great magician uncovered a spell that hurries sweet moments of forgiveness:

Take a needle and carefully prick the flesh over your heart. Write in blood on a clean piece of white silk your name and your lover's name, written in the smallest letters possible. Now draw (in ash) a circle around your names. Fold the silk up, and at the first sight of the evening star, bury it in the earth. As soon as it's buried, you may expect your lover to have no peace until he sees you and makes up. But tell no one about your spell, or it won't work, and may even turn him permanently against you.

Happily, this same charm may also be made by a man. He should prick his little finger for the blood, however, not the flesh over his heart. In either case, don't forget to apply the proper pitch of emotion and concentration when making the charm.

There's no way, but *no* way, to get back a man who's lost interest in you without the aid of witchcraft. I personally feel that if a man loses interest, it's probably best to just let him go without hassling him too much to come back. The odds are he won't, anyway, but if he does, it's likely he'll only lose interest again and double your troubles.

But some girls get psychologically addicted to men and will go to great lengths to put off the agony of finally having to give them up. Never mind the psychiatric aspects of such relationships; a girl hurts, but badly, if she's that hung up and is rejected. As with drugs, a sharp break can be more painful than a slower withdrawal. The emotional system has a chance to shake itself out, to get its knots of need untied, to get used to the pain, if the end is put off a bit.

There are plenty of lonely, bluesy nights for a girl who gets walking papers and never dreamed she'd get them. She's a pure mess, her heart so mashed that a mere mental picture of the man puts her in bed with the vapors. There's no such thing as hope, or going on without him. This is a dangerous time—sleeping pills are carefully hoarded, kitchen knives get sharpeneed, window-to-ground distances are estimated, midnight walks to bridges are contemplated—and there should be some way to fan back to life even one spark of hope that may have survived.

There is such a way, a spell that provides the possibility of actually having a love back. Whether it works out for the best or not, the knowledge that a man's feelings can be changed so he'll return is hope enough for any half-dead woman.

Stick a needle through the wick of a candle. Light it, concentrate, and speak the following incantation:

> Needle in the flame, needle of fire,
> Pierce his thoughts,
> Make him writhe, agonize,
> Till his heart turns back to me.

Horrors. Something perfectly dreadful is happening to your idyllic love affair, and you haven't a clue what it is. He comes into your apartment and, almost as an afterthought, gives you one of those unattractive, dry, chapped-lip kisses. On the cheek. He sits on the couch and is instantly engrossed in the new issue of *Playboy*. That he brought with him. You hand him a drink and ask what kind of a day he's had, and he says "Ummm."

Could it be bad breath? Is your deodorant failing? Maybe

your see-through shirt isn't see-throughable enough? Or is there another woman? Whatever it is, your relationship has definitely turned middle-aged, and it's time to decide how you really feel about him.

If you admit to yourself that this whole *Playboy*-ummm-worry-and-soul-searching bit is faintly boring, you're about to bring on your bowing-out routine ("I'm so sorry I can't make it this weekend—a friend's asked me to Acapulco"). But what if you find you really can't be happy without the man, and you're going to be utterly devastated if there really *is* another girl?

It's a crisis situation, and it calls for strong measures. First, get your spy network going and find out if he *is* seeing someone else. At the same time, muster all your cool and figure out some amusing things to do—perhaps *you're* boring *him*. If your feminine charm and your wile can't rouse him, and if your spy network produces rumblings but nothing specific, then try the following spell:

> Sew a little cloth doll to resemble your lover. Make the clothes for it in a brilliant shade of red velvet. Put a gold wedding band (never used) on its left arm. Now take it to a church, and hide it behind the altar itself, if that is possible, or in its vicinity, such as in the choir loft. Your love should be permanently attached to you almost at once; but follow directions carefully, or he won't propose marriage—just a ménage à deux.

There's always the possibility, you know, that the man you fall in love with won't be one of those marvelous creatures who become so hypnotically engrossed in a girl's charms that they send flowers on frequent whims. There's every chance, in fact, that your love will be an independent man—the sort who disappears for weekends at his friend's ranch in Canada, and sometimes doesn't call even to say hello for days on end. He's the man who hangs you up with wondering. He's always reassuring you, always earnest about being in love with you—when he's around. But *how*, you're forever asking yourself, can he love you when he's *away* so much!

Yes, actions usually are a better guide to someone's feelings than words are, but when you're in love and blind to danger you become convinced that maxims and generalizations about human behavior just don't apply in your case. So you accept and accept, and let him get away with what you're not able to see as outrageous mistreatment (that he spends all his winter weekends skiing in Aspen while you pine away at home doesn't bother you?). Such selfish inconsideration from a man who professes to be in love! Face up to it, and you may suddenly realize that you're being used.

If you're able to get yourself out of your love daze long enough to see the truth, and if you don't flip out with anger —and even decide he's worth the trouble to bring to heel —then the following charm will help solve your trouble. Wherever he may be roaming, it will bring him home (use this spell in combination with a heavy love charm, and he'll fly into your arms forever).

Take a needle and prick your wrist with it, and write in blood on parchment your first name and your lover's last. Then draw a square around the names and carry the parchment over your heart. He'll be home within a week.

It must be one of those quirky laws of nature that makes it always happen. But isn't it true that every single time you take a vacation or visit a friend in another city, the ugly man that you inevitably meet lives just down the block from you, and the attractive one invariably comes from some wholly inaccessible place—such as California if you're a New Yorker, or France if you're from Utah? He always is the one you fall in love with, too, and you just know you could spend the rest of your life tending and spoiling him. But usually in a few days or weeks he's gone for good. Oh, you write letters once or twice, but then your better judgment counsels you to cool it, and your emotions spring back into shape. You label the affair a romantic interlude, part of the shifting pattern of full, rich experiences that fill out your interesting life.

Of course if you have a great deal of loose money in your checking account you can always go visit the marvelous man. (Although a friend of mine did this, and spent a year tracking him around the Continent, with the result that she came home exhausted, broke, and with a battered heart. And an English friend followed a Swiss lover to this country several months after he'd come here, only to discover he'd married a Southern belle two weeks before she arrived.) It's terribly important, if you're rich, that you know exactly who your man is and how he feels about you before you give in to your compulsion to follow him.

Much easier, by far, and the safer emotional route, is to get this wonder lover to pay *you* a visit. Immediately you know he must care about you if he comes, and any tracking about this continent will be done by him in hot pursuit of exciting you. You have him just where you want him—on your terms. How do you get this man, you ask, to visit from some remote land, when by all odds the affair should be a sweet memory by Tuesday? Very simple:

> Put salt on your doorstep, and over the door frame, too, each day for a fortnight. Your lover will come to you shortly thereafter.

✍ A Fidelity Test ࿇

Within a very few decades, it seems, vows of chastity will be obsolete. Priests are agitating to abolish the celibacy laws of the Catholic church so that they can marry or have lovers if they wish. Chastity among the young and unmarried is no longer required by society (just the youth society, to be sure, but these mores will, no doubt, eventually prevail). Fewer and fewer married couples are abiding by their vows of chastity, as adulterous affairs become more the rule than the exception. Virginal fidelity to an idea or individual just isn't popular any more.

It may be that future marriages—if they're still called that —will be conducted more like the old-fashioned Continental marriages. Men will have lovers; this time, however, women will have them, too—but it will all be open and free. Jealousy, as a reaction to infidelity, won't even enter into the picture.

Meanwhile, we continue to protect our vested love interests in each other, and the monster with green eyes breathes rage into us if we feel betrayed. We're not ready yet to deal with the idea that the emotion of love can be separate from the stirrings of lust (although men have, since the year one, been very nicely practicing this division of feeling). So what do we do about jealousy? Continue to express it, of course (although our great-grandchildren probably won't).

So you're not feeling exactly sure about what your lover is up to, right? You think he may be hung up on someone else, yet you don't really know. Here's a fine Oriental fidelity test that will help you divine the score:

Light a stick of incense and hold it up straight. If the incense remains lit, and the ash doesn't fall for three minutes, all is well. Otherwise, he's up to something, for sure.

⋖§ Getting Even §⋗

There are few experiences quite so devastating as having your heart stomped on. How could it have happened to me? you say. You were so careful—timidly entering the garden of love one pink toe at a time, and searching that paradise methodically for any nasty, prickly thorns hiding among the roses. And *still* you got pricked. You trusted him; he betrayed you.

What makes a man so devilishly cruel? you ask. Why in the name of heaven does he bother with you in the first place if he intends to drop you in the middle—just after he's convinced you that his garden's roses are the prettiest you'll ever see? There he was vowing his undying love to you last night, and there he is today on the beach trying to score with a wretched brunette. What kind of a kick does he get from such treachery, anyhow?

Oh, for revenge! Yes, wouldn't it be nice if you could get him back just long enough to stomp on *his* heart. It probably wouldn't be quite so awaful for you if the brunette were really pretty, with lots of dimples and gentle curves like you have. But she's chubby! And that makes you twice as angry. Your best shot at tying the score lies in re-seducing him.

But how do you accomplish that? First, get yourself together and disguise your broken heart and your scorn. You must appear convincing. Stand in front of a mirror and practice a distant, mysterious smile to use when you next see him. There's nothing like an aura of mystery to attract a wandering man. Turn down any dates he might ask you on, but show up at places he's likely to be—with someone else, if you can. If not, just show up and flirt a lot with everyone there except him. He'll be hurt, curious, and hooked.

To ensure that you'll both turn up at the same place at the same time so you can work your charms on him, do the following spell before going to bed.

Light a candle of white wax and look deep into the flame. Concentrate as hard as you can while visualizing him, and chant over and over:

> I my love I wish to see,
> Bring him where I plan to be.

I have yet to see it fail. Everytime you knit a man something—especially an item such as a sweater that requires a great deal of work—he suddenly breaks up with you. And it's usually just when you're doing the ribbing at the neck, or sewing the seams. Ah, the urge to spit. But you usually give in, don't you, and give the rat the sweater anyway because who *else*, on earth, is seven feet six and can wear the thing?

Argyle socks are deadly, too. This knitting of socks went on with me through two broken hearts, until I got wise. Both pairs of socks were supposed to be Christmas gifts, which is a doubly deadly combination: we all know that men break up with you just before Christmas or New Year's Eve.

So if you have unwisely knitted your man a gift and now find him sliding out your door, restrain yourself, put your handiwork in mothballs, and give him a little something else to remember you by.

There are a certain number of gifts that you can give to a man that will bring him bad luck. Here they are:

    a coin case
    a locket with your picture in it
    a tie tack
    a cigar clipper
    a cigarette lighter
    a painted portrait (of you)
    a tie, a wool cap, a silk ascot
    a keyring
    a nail from a horseshoe
    a peacock feather
    a quill pen

These are bad-luck flowers to give: poppies, geraniums, Jack-in-the-pulpits, jonquils, all red flowers, all strongly scented perfumes.

❧ *Arousing His Lust* ☙

Advocates of women's sexual emancipation are busy these days telling us that it's perfectly normal for healthy young girls to want men, and, what's more, it's perfectly acceptable to sleep with them provided you first take the pill. You don't even have to be in love with them any more. Grandma's wildest secret dreams have come true, and today's uptight, middle-aged mothers are downright jealous!

It seems, however, that before the age of Victoria and frigid women, happy peasant girls were enticing country fellows with magical charms that induced no-holds-barred lust. It's hard to believe, with the foggy-bottom mist of Victorian moral thought still around us, that there was a time when lust wasn't banished and booed to death. That girls actually solicited such attention seems inconceivable. Yet the contemporary girl's attitudes on sex are closer to those of the ladies of Louis XIV's court than to her own grandmother's, and, more than likely, her mother's. It seems a shame that we have to fight over again sexual battles that were, by and large, won once. (That's not to say, however, that in every age there haven't been masses of little black-swathed ladies running around shaking their fingers and tch-tching at nubile young things.)

Here is one charm used by the happy peasant girls to attract lascivious attentions from willing males:

Find a whole sea shell on the beach (shells are a female sex symbol). Take it home with you and concentrate for a week on it while visualizing him. Then arrange to hide it in his bedroom (under his bed is the best place), and wait for him to run breathlessly into your arms.

✑ *If You Think You're Pregnant* ... ও✎

So you think you're going to have a baby! If you're married, you're probably keeping your fingers, toes, and legs crossed and are rejoicing over the prospect. If you're not married...

Have you rocked any empty cradles lately? Or stepped on the shadow of a child? Perhaps you accidentally stroked the fur of a male cat backwards, or spilled milk in an empty room! Anyway, as certain as an empty cradle should never be rocked or it soon will be filled, you've gone and done it, and you're writhing around agonizing over what to do next.

There are many answers, these days, to your problem. You can jump out the window. You can get a hospital board to predict you'll probably have a mental collapse if you have a baby. You can find an old crone or a midwife or a shady doctor through a friend of a friend of a friend; they'll give you an abortion, but it could be with a knitting needle or a dirty scalpel. You could be lucky and live in New York. Or you can even keep the child these days (the groovy thing to do in some circles), and people will applaud your independence, or at the risk of looking square, at least more or less keep their scorn to themselves. Yes, there are lots of options for you.

But before you decide which course to take, perhaps you'll consider doing what English girls do. Assuming you haven't been to the doctor yet, all you really know is that your period's very late.

To bring on your period, bind your body about with red

and white strands of silk thread, using one spool of each color. Now sit in a tub of water containing essences of rose, orange, wisteria, and jasmine in equal parts. Stay in the bath till the threads disentangle themselves from your body, naturally, then let the threads drain out with the bath water. Using proper magical concentration, your condition can be nipped in the bud. (Personally, I recommend contraceptives.)

Yes, modern contraceptives have changed society. They can be credited with the emergence of a new woman—an unmarried, emancipated woman. Instead of cowering around wondering if next month will prove that she's going to be a mother, this new woman can, without inwardly knit brows, actually carry on an affair, sure that it won't die an untimely death through pregnancy. She can be in *love* with no worried reservations. And with the threatening voices of priests and preachers screeching about sin reduced to barely audible whispers these days, our new woman in a generation or so may even have lost her ungodly sense of guilt. That's all very fine for the new woman.

But what about the retiring flowers who walk around with their eyes shut, unborn inside the closed bud of social conformity? These are the girls to watch out for (and there are millions more of them than the emancipated variety). They're the old-fashioned ones who think contraceptives are unromantic. They're the ones who would rather risk having a child (it-could-never-happen-to-me types) than do anything so distasteful as use contraceptive measures; they'd have to admit, then, there was a need to take precautions. And these girls are nothing but certain that they're basically virginal—with, perhaps, an occasional lapse. But the lapses aren't real to them. And in the lapse lies the danger.

For young ladies who can't conceive of being pregnant, here's an old Italian peasant spell to find out if it might (**horrors**) be true after all:

Pluck from a white hen ten white feathers. Now carefully draw blood from your left wrist and touch the tip of each quill in the blood. Take the feathers outdoors, at noon, to a spot where it is neither too windy nor too still and set them out in a circle, with the quill ends pointing in. Now make a circle around the feathers (close to them) with salt, and sit down nearby to wait. Concentrate on the feathers, visualizing them forever protected from the wind by the magic salt circle. If night falls and none of the feathers has moved, you're in luck. You're not pregnant. However, if, during the course of the afternoon, the wind blows one or more of the feathers outside the magic circle, then you're in blessed circumstances. (Wow! Not even the pill can help you now.)

◄§ If You Are Pregnant... ξ►

We practice witchcraft on ourselves in small ways all the time. "I can't go out tonight after all, Robert. I'm so tired I can hardly sit up." The realities of an evening spent with poor, boring Robert just drained the energy out of you. "I'd love to cook that fancy dinner I promised you tonight, but I seem to have the most fantastic headache." Since when have you loved to cook, and a fancy dinner at that? "I'm getting a cold and I feel I shouldn't risk coming to work today. Sorry I can't write up that report I promised." It was only a morning sneeze, but the thought of that miserable report sure enough turned it into a real cold later in the day. It's well known that wives in perfect physical condition can subsconsciously keep themselves from becoming pregnant. It's also quite possible to have a false pregnancy—with real childbirth pains—and no baby.

Some people call it psychosomatic or the power of suggestion, others say it's using mind over matter; but the physical retreats we create for ourselves are bewitchments, pure and simple. That part of the mind which in magic projects our will on others can also enact strange physical changes in us.

It is certain that in some ways ancient peoples better understood our mysterious minds than we will for some time to come. It's their perception of the mind's power that makes the following belief on abortion comprehensible:

> If you're unhappily pregnant and go to a grave wherein a witch is buried, and say a prayer backwards in front of that grave, you'll have a miscarriage.

Such an abortion works, of course, only for girls who attribute some power to witches and witchcraft. The mind focuses with the help of these dark symbols on the destruction of the fetus. If its work is interrupted by passing thoughts such as: ". . . this is *ridiculous* . . . what can saying a prayer backwards do," then it's certain that the baby will survive.

Have you any idea how much *work* a baby is? Consider the responsibility of rearing offspring. Who says they won't turn out to be wastrels or ungrateful? And yet mothers continue to have babies without so much as a fearful glance over their shoulders.

For that matter, think of the streams of men and women who, without stopping to consider what their lovers might be like at 8 a.m. or on a stretch of quiet evenings at home, continue to get married. Does anyone ever really pause to think what this getting married and having babies business is all about? Of course not. Nature veils the meaning of these remarkable life-changing actions with euphoria, a sense of well-being, just as, conversely, it masks unbearable pain with unconsciousness. It can be truly said that innocence of marriage and having babies is bliss. Innocence of the fearful odds against a project—be it working on an invention which will change the world, or creating babies—can sometimes make way for genius.

If you're pregnant and intend to have the baby, you probably want to bear a genius (if for no better reason than to make *you* look good), but what variety are you going to have—boy or girl? As people have been pondering this same question for a good many centuries, it's not surprising that the gypsies found a way to divine an infant's sex:

> Go into a garden where there are red and white rose bushes growing closely together. Spin around in front of the bushes eleven times with your eyes shut, moving from east to west, then reach out and pick one of the rose blooms. If you've chosen a white one, you'll have a girl, if a red one, a boy.

⤐§ *If You Would Like to Be Pregnant* §⤐

There is entirely too much childbearing going on, especially now when marriage patterns are changing. Experts tell us that in a hundred years there won't be enough food to feed the multitudes of human beings who will be alive then; there will be massive starvation everywhere—Biafra on an earthwide scale.

Why, with Famine's specter hovering so near, do we continue to tolerate religious beliefs that so recklessly (and injuriously to everyone) deny the wide-scale use of contraceptives? Which is more immoral: to prevent the conception of a baby, or to allow that seedling its humanity so that it may die an agonizing death in hunger? (Take a deep breath and count to ten.)

Furthermore, it's unconscionable that couples bear children in the first few years of marriage. All too often, just as the baby is born, the marriage ends in divorce.

However, if you feel a need for having children, and have somehow been struck infertile, there is a charm which is said to be a cure for your condition. To bring on pregnancy, borrow a diaper from a friend who has young children. Tie the diaper around you, as you would a bikini bottom, then slip a moonstone charm down the front of it. Go to bed, and before falling asleep, concentrate on having a child soon.

CHAPTER II

Aphrodisiacs

There is nothing more stimulating, or euphoria-making, than love. How appropriate that just the sound of the word *aphrodisiac* produces euphoria! Every sense comes alert in the company of a lover, every nerve twitches with anticipation. The heart drowns in a sea of sweet longing. How sad that for many lovers quivers and shivers and thrilling encounters are lost in a matter of time.

It's almost inevitable, however, when mysteries lie revealed, when lovers' unknown depths are plumbed, that heartbeats quicken less readily. But in what fantastic greener pastures man has sought the palpitating pulse! How many sultans have collected glittering odalisques by the haremful, whose whole work was their pleasure? How many Druse girls have been specially raised to fulfill the lusty needs of Arab men? How many Westerners have changed wives or taken on mistresses in pursuit of sparkling emotion? For that matter, how many wives have changed husbands or acquired lovers for the same reason? In the thrall of familiarity, how many people have sought to recapture at least some of the old excitement with special herbs and magic concoctions?

Many, many, many. Rather than throw over beloved hus-

41

bands, wives, or lovers for the excitement of newer mates, people in every age, around the world, have relied on stimulating aphrodisiacs. From the beginning, the aphrodisial arts were linked with magic; the most efficacious mixtures were always sold by local crones, sorcerers, or medicine men. Times have changed little, for in the botanicas of upper Manhattan they're still mixed for the local populace by adepts. What's significant, however, is that in every stratum of our non-magic-oriented society, interest in magic aphrodisiacs is growing. Recently, an aphrodisiac cookbook became extraordinarily popular, proving again just how widespread the trend is toward accepting ancient ideas and practices in our new times.

The huge body of writing about aphrodisiacs, magic and otherwise, is, to say the least, confusing to sort out and make sense of. Modern medicine has confirmed that some of the ancient recipes work—usually those based on plants that have natural narcotic properties. But who's to say that many of the now scorned aphrodisiacs really didn't work for the Greeks, the Romans, and everyone else? It's perfectly reasonable to me that if Penelope tells Odysseus there's some magic mandrake in his wine, pretty soon he's going to start feeling glowy all over and enchanted with the flirtatious tendrils of her dark hair.

It's a shame that doctors have to be so cut-and-dried about the effects of potions on the body. They never give credit to the psychology of using them—the same psychology that they do concede can turn a healthy individual into a disease-ridden wraith.

Never mind. There's room for everyone, especially for those of us who feel intuitively that beyond pure scientific knowledge there is other truth: that each individual is as different as a snowflake, with a special combination of brain cells that puts his powers beyond the generalities of ordinary scientific ken. If we believe that a magical charm or aphrodisiac works, and it *does*, we are entitled to thumb our noses at the rigid scientific and medical establishment. They're only at the threshold of learning, anyway, and in an astonishing array of cases are fumbling about discovering medicines to cure ills for which they've yet to find causes.

Let us be thankful for modern medicine, however, and charitable about its pomposities and frailties; we'll go on about our business with gusto. The romance of aphrodisiacs, and the sure belief they work, will bring us satisfaction and success.

⋞ Seducing Him ⋟

Suppose you are in a slow period now; you've just ended a long, lovely relationship that was beginning to sour. You've been out of circulation for months, and you don't know *anyone* any more. If you are a man, your social stride will hardly be broken before an amusing girl turns up—on the beach, at a singles bar, at a rock concert. If you are a girl, the pause can quickly become a social-life gap (unless, of course, you start hanging about the beach, the singles bars, and rock concerts).

Whatever your *modus operandi* after the big breakup, it seems likely that only part of you is going to be concentrating on meeting new people. The rest of you will be untying all the little knotted strands of involvement left over from your affair—like disassociating your old lover's presence from your favorite haunts, for example.

Wouldn't it be lovely if, during this emotionally exhausted time, you could take out some insurance on future dates with someone? Like that intriguing-looking person you just met? While you don't have the heart for making meaningful contact now, you *know* you could be interested. Follow directions for the aphrodisiacal love charm that follows, and you'll have that insurance (you've got double indemnity, please note, with magic and the aphrodisiac combined).

Concoct a brew of equal parts of sugar, mashed lilies-of-the-valley, and gingerroot. While you mash this to a pulp, say over and over to yourself:

> He to me and I to he
> As one we ever shall be.

Now put your charm in a vial, and at the first opportunity, put a pinch into a prospect's food or drink. Be sure you use proper concentration in making the aphrodisiac and popping it in his food or drink, or it won't have its full, interesting effect.

I know a girl who's something of a witch and a confirmed believer in, and user of, magic aphrodisiacs. She's extremely attractive, in her twenties, and hardly needs to employ aphrodisiacs for traditional reasons. However, she tells me, she starts feeding them right away to any man who catches her fancy as a potential lover—to ensure his continuing interest in her. She's not insecure about being able to have lasting relationships with men, she says, but as all is fair in love and war, the aphrodisiac gives her the edge, the advantage, over her man. I agree with her point. All magic is used to give one some kind of extra control or power.

My friend says she always has a dish of cherry tomatoes among the hors d'oeuvres she serves with drinks when she has a special guest. The legend is that these tiny tomatoes are powerful love titillators (they're also called love apples). However potent cherry tomatoes may be, I can't vouch for them, as Scotch and tomato don't mix well in my book.

As for dinner. If my friend is particularly interested in her male guest, she says she serves him a dish of fried peppers and pimento which has, for extra kick, chocolate-covered ants mixed in. This girl's so serious about the efficacy of ants, she shuns the gourmet counters where you can *buy* the things, and chocolate-coats her own from scratch.

With after-dinner coffee and brandy, my friend says she puts out a dish of marijuana leaves (she grows her own). That's if she wishes to seduce her guest on the spot (aggressive little thing!). She goes in for opium and waterpipes, too, so I guess she knows whereof she speaks when it comes to wild love trips. Once she mentioned other, more potent, drugs which are also spectacularly aphrodisial, but she'd only hint at them, and definitely didn't tell me how to use them. Certain American mushrooms to be found in any woods, and a certain weed that grows on Cape Cod. Too dangerous for most people to try, she says. I believe her.

It might be a good idea if you started carrying some prepared aphrodisiac powders around with you (don't groan, just buy a bigger handbag). You just never know whom you're going to meet suddenly—James Brown; Blood, Sweat and Tears; Philip Roth, who knows? Being a witch, you most certainly want to be prepared.

Disguise your magic aphrodisiacs so that, when the moment is opportune, you can give them to your subject without having him ask you too many embarrassing questions. For example, learn to make mints, adding your powder, of course, and carry a packet with you at all times. Should you find yourself on a rainy night standing about under an umbrella with a fascinating man, offer him some mints. Almost everybody eats mints.

Empty some tiny time-pill capsules and refill them with magic aphrodisiac. Everyone's a pillhead these days, and should your lovely man sneeze—even once—whip out your remedy. Say it's a super anti-cold pill, and he sounds like he's getting a bad one.

If he's got chapped lips, dry hands, or peeling sunburn, flash your pills and say the dermatologist gave them to you to take for your chapped lips, dry hands, or peeling sunburn. Some kind of marvelous vitamins. They practically cured your condition overnight. Could he resist?

If you're addicted to the natural narcotics scene, keep some with you—practically no one these days would turn down the offer of a plant high (chemical highs, yes, because they sound lots more dangerous). Most narcotic plants are multi-aphrodisiacal (just don't remind him of that fact).

One of the best aphrodisiacs to encapsulate or make in mints is one suggested by an English magician of the thirteenth century: the shed skin of a snake pulverized to a fine degree (see your local wholesale snakeskin dealer for some; boutiques are using snake like mad this year, so there is a lot of it everywhere). He says add it to sack, but if you're on the street or at the movies, stick with a more practical drink. (Don't forget to concentrate as you pulverize the snakeskin.)

Sometimes it's necessary to go on a no-holds-barred campaign to seduce the man you're after. It may be that he's been bringing himself up as one of those ultra-cool New York-type bachelors who, it sometimes seems, only marry in moments of supreme weakness, or if a girl's father is willing to make them vice president in the family firm. Such men, if they're attractive, are usually surrounded by brigades of willing lovers, and generally can't conceive of marriage much before they reach fifty. What a bore. But if you're absolutely certain you want to get mixed up with a man this spoiled (and usually pompous), and if your father isn't about to make him vice president of anything, then there's nothing for it but to set about catching him.

And catch him you will have to. Like the equally elusive

California species, your New York *Homo sapiens* must be pampered and coddled and generally treated as if he'd just stepped down from Mount Olympus to grace you with his presence. (Have you considered spinsterhood?) None of your soft, feminine attentions are going to have, by themselves, the least effect on him, you understand: your man's harem treats him with equal tenderness. But do the coddling routine if you want him, for it's still a major move in the catch-him game.

Naturally, you must know how (and somehow afford) to dress beautifully, and how to say funny things to amuse him. Your competition is stiff; if you're not up to the basics (sophisticated coddling, clothes, and charm), you may not, quite honestly, get him. (How lovely it must be to live in a commune and forget this phony husband-luring scene!)

But if you still want to persevere, and can handle the glamorous bits, this next aphrodisiac—properly prepared with your attention riveted on his image—should clinch him for you:

> Take a pinch of ambergris, half a pinch of musk, and twelve apple seeds. Grind these ingredients together in a mortar and add to seven ounces of red wine. Now boil this mixture down till it's three-quarters evaporated, and pour the results in a stoppered bottle. Use it sparingly in such foods as clear consommé, or a sweet drink such as pineapple juice, or cocktails like Pink Ladies and Banana Daiquiris.

The best way to live, some girls say, is just to have as many men as you like, without getting seriously involved with any of them. These girls believe that if you have a passel of them with whom you regularly go out drinking or smoking and who take you to dinner and the movies and the theater and the galleries and around, you not only get yourself about a good deal, you have compatible lovers when you want them. Such a situation does seem idyllic, if you genuinely like them all and have a lovely relationship with each one—friendly, warm, giving.

What usually happens, however, is that you find yourself engaged in a non-friendly bartering game with your lovers. They'll take you to the movies, or out for some drinks or something, if they can come back and sleep with you later— that sort of thing. This is a decidedly untenable state of affairs for you, unless you're the sort of woman who more than anything else wants to go to the movies or the theater and is then happy to exchange her charms for the gala evening out. It's more likely, however, that you'll feel you've got the bad end of a bad bargain. Your charms, you're certain, are worth more than five dollars in beer at the local pub.

That's why it's much nicer to have some love on the scene, so that you don't feel as if your life is a wasteful round of giving too much and receiving too little. If there is some genuine feeling involved with your relationships, then evenings spent with your various men can be worthwhile, relaxed, and pleasurable, and you won't feel left short when you sleep with them.

To evoke love in your lovers, use this magic aphrodisiac:

> Make a mixture of one part lemon oil and one part patchouli. Add the mixture to six parts of alcohol and add a few leaves of rue. Take a nice hot bath so you're pink and steamy, then rub on the perfume. Your men will always find you intriguing and lovable.

⨳ *Protecting Your Sexiness* ⨳

Lots of the classic aphrodisiac recipes from the witches and magicians of the fourteenth and fifteenth centuries are, as might be expected, nothing but nasty. I don't personally believe you have to get into human excrement to make a perfectly serviceable magic aphrodisiac, but there are modern purist witches who feel you do. My theory is that the power that makes all magic work is a form of ESP; it's focused and heightened when directed through potions and spells. However, classicists feel that the ingredients used in potions and charms are efficacious in themselves because they give off certain vibrations; you help focus the vibrations with incantations and strong emotion.

Thus, ancient love philtres are often composed of such hideous substances as bits of dead human bodies. No ingredients in magic, purists believe, are as potent as human flesh and blood—especially if the owner of them died a violent death. The agony, fear, and hate of the dying person (usually a child) are retained in his body material and passed along in the potion.

One English love philtre dating from the 1400s is made by combining such elements as the left index finger of a hanged man (taken while his body is still warm and swinging aloft) cut up and mixed with wormwood. The powerful vibrations in this tasty morsel are meant to ensure potency, and, apparently, prolong the sweet agonies of love.

Only slightly less revolting is a classic philtre for preserving your own sexual capacities should the spells of some fiendish witch you may happen to know be suddenly cast on you. A sorcerer and alchemist who lived in the 1600s recommended brewing tea to which was added some drops of menstrual blood collected from a virgin. Presumably you could then sip this mixture with your evening meal and live (hopefully) well preserved ever after.

One of the great human experiences is the sweet engulfing euphoria, the laughing, rippling, softly drifting sensation of sexual union born of sensitive, trusting love. Physical love, then, is happy, a part of loving the other's being, a being inside or taking the other into you, a warm haven, a safe harbor.

And while this perfect union is within the grasp of all lovers, it is, sadly, not always theirs. Fears that surround the giving of love are mountain-high, and to have such love is to trust the love of another, to know that it's real. You must feel truly loved. It's not a matter of being afraid that the others' love for you will end. It's simply feeling completely loved during the course of the affair's moment. And your lover must feel that you love him, too, in the same way, as he can be free to love you only if he's free of fear.

If doubt is the enemy of the perfect love union, then doubt we must eliminate. And since evil vibrations are always at work trying to cause this mental ailment, we must be prepared for them. Before you receive your lover, make this perfume and burn it in your bedchamber:

Take powdered musk, salt, civet, and bits of sandal-wood, and mix them carefully together. Add the petals of orange blossoms and roses, which you've dried into a potpourri. Now consecrate your perfume before using it with the following words:

O Lord of the Heavens, the Earth,
The great waters of the Sea,
Sanctify this perfume
So that anyone who breathes it
Will be cleansed of evil thoughts and intentions,
And dream only of love.
Consecrate the flowers of the scent
So that a devil who breathes their odors
Can make no mischief.
This I beseech you,
Oh Lord of the great Heaven
And Earth
And Seas.

Have your love without a care.

With all the publicity surrounding the modern woman and her carefree sex life, you'd think that this newsy creature had just arrived on the scene fullblown—Venus reborn in the 1970s. It's as if a whole generation (the news media would have us believe) had taken leave of its mothers' good, old-fashioned sense, and, en masse, is now walking braless, de-Victorianized and demoralized, through the cities and suburbs of our land. What utter nonsense. There are just as many nymphets wearing unlockable chastity belts of motherly admonition today as there ever have been. They're just not talking—it's not *chic* to have sexual hangups.

Enjoy, enjoy. Yes, indeed. No doubt there are thousands of young women overcoming fearful guilt and actually enjoying sex. But there are millions more, you can believe it, who are losing the guilt battle but grinning nevertheless—*actresses*, just like their mothers. The difference is that the new women hate every frigid minute of the grand sham—unlike their mothers, who equated unaroused sexuality with respectability.

What unfortunate creatures these frigid "emancipated" women are. While their mothers never expected sexual satisfaction and therefore weren't disappointed when they didn't get it, the modern frigid girl *expects* to be satisfied; furthermore, when she isn't, she daren't tell anyone about her problem. It isn't fashionable today to be frigid.

Psychiatry, of course, is usually the answer for such troubles, but psychiatry is expensive; our modern emancipated woman is usually young and can't afford it. What to do? One of our greatest modern witches suggests taking the herb Verbena and wearing it in a white satin pouch about the neck (she attributes increased sexual desire to the herb). The trick here, of course, is that if you *know* the amulet is going to work, is *really* (regardless of your guilt) going to open floodgates of desire—if you believe in it—it will work. Frigidity (as every good witch knows) is all in the mind.

✑ *Insuring Your Interests* ⇖

I believe in insuring myself against failure as much as possible. When undertaking a new study, such as magic potions, the odds are more against successfully applying them than for it, until enough time and energy have been spent on experimentation to slide the odds to the favorable end of the scale.

This holds true with making magic aphrodisiacs. You must try a few just to get the hang of how they're made and used, and then learn a few tricks to doubly insure yourself against failure at critical moments.

Suppose you've had the good fortune to meet and fall in love with a spectacular man. And suppose that you've invited him to your apartment, where you plan to apply some magical persuasion to ensure a love affair. If I were you, I'd certainly escalate the probabilities by picking out a love charm or two to work, making up some potent magic aphrodisiac, and then planning a menu of aphrodisiacal foods to triply invoke his loving thoughts.

For the main course at dinner, consider serving one of these dishes, as they encourage venereal strength: boeuf stroganoff, rack of baby lamb, pheasant under glass, goose with mushroom dressing, or Long Island duckling. Mussels might be fun to have with fresh bean salad and a honeyed dessert such as baklava (Mediterranean peoples have long used honey as a restorative). Shellfish, or perhaps something amusing (but hard to get) like conch, are aphrodisiacal. Whatever you have, be sure to garnish it with lots of truffles, considered to be one of the finest stimulation foods since early Roman times, when they were often served at orgies.

Onions, eggs, and coconut all induce sweet languor, as does that most phallic fruit, the banana. Green onions, cauliflower, and wine (of course) have a similar effect, and one extravagant ancient recipe recommends shaving off bits of amber and adding them to oil and honey for a potent drink (give it to him in the morning, should he stay over). Another nice refreshing drink, especially as a nightcap before bedtime, is a cup of very thick honey mixed with the fruit of the date palm and pine nuts (watch this—pine nuts, to some people, act like ragweed). A few white peppercorns, or a stick of cinnamon chewed, have a galvanizing effect, as does a mixture of white wine and nettle seed (ouch!).

Some of the Middle Eastern and Oriental aphrodisiacs are, as you might expect, among the most potent in the world. There's the Turkish poppy that grows on the hillsides around Istanbul (European heads vouch for it). Musk and ambergris, taken in small quantities, also lengthen love trips (again, experts concur). To bring on the proper mood for dalliance, dab some musk behind your ears (even if you *look* like a witch, no man could resist you).

Bhang, the favored aphrodisiac of India, consists of hemp seeds, which are sometimes chewed for a long, colorful, tranquil high—the effect is not unlike that of hashish, the classic aphrodisiac. Japan's favorite root is *ninjin*, and in Korea and China, it's ginseng (comb New York's Chinatown, or inquire at a groovy pharmacy for the latter). Our own Western cantharides (Spanish Fly) is among the finest aphrodisiacs known (but be very wary of the dosage, as too much produces convulsions, and the most agonizing death, in a misery of twitching pains).

If you really intend to go at it, the thoughtful thing to do is to have a few external remedies on hand for your over-indulged man. If you're serving him Long Island duckling for dinner, save the grease and add to it small quantities of honey, curry powder, and sugar, along with a few drops of orange or jasmine essence for perfume. When he's limp with fatigue, he'll appreciate your liniment. A mixture of cloves (powdered), ginger, olive oil, and freshly ground pepper also makes a stimulating, revivifying salve.

However, during the course of the night, should *you* become painfully aware that you've over-indulged, and there's no sign that your lover has had his fill, you might consider mixing up a batch of *an*aphrodisiac to cool his fervor. (Such an underhanded trick, as you must know, should be approached with diplomacy—don't tell him what he's really drinking, or he'll be so turned off he'll leave in a huff.)

No man would suspect the side effects of a large glass of cola (you could even tell him it's for his strength and not be fibbing). Freshly squeezed fruit juices, or any whole fruit with a high acid content, will cool him down, as will plain icy water.

If you wish to be fancy about your anaphrodisiacs, some effective gourmet potions may be made by crushing the waters from ordinary salad greens or, more exquisitely, gardenias, in an electric blender. (How paradoxically romantic. There you are in your summery penthouse apartment, and at sunrise you drift across your terrace to pick fresh blossoms from a gardenia tree. With these you make a potion to kill his passion. Witches sometimes have to do these things.) White carnations are also anaphrodisiacal, and they may be crushed for their juices, or added whole to a snifter of ice water (how decorative, he'll think). You can also mix orange and lemon juice, add sections of grapefruit and ripe red cherries for a fragrant, devastating nectar, or if you really feel energetic, pick some sassafras leaves and brew a strong tea from them. Mustard seeds added to peach juice give it an extra zing (it will also take the zing out of him), as will a refreshing cup of thick, black espresso.

If some combination of these anaphrodisiacs won't cool

him, he's probably a Casanova and nothing short of deep analysis, or a powerful magic spell, will make the slightest dent in his ardor. You're stuck with him—unless, of course, you mention he's been fed a lot of anaphrodisiacs. Then he'll surely take the hint and go!

What could possibly be more delightful, in our busy times, than to have two or three days to spend any way you like with the man you love? Imagine disappearing to a moon- and sun-swept beach somewhere, where a comfortable house, filled with amenities, lies forever in the thrall of surf and seabird music. Here's a place to escape to, where no one but the two of you is around to disturb the summer nights with laughter.

Or imagine some quiet pond in a wood with a little house and wild flowers all about, and the sounds of cicadas at noon and thrushes trilling in the dusk. Here you could loll for hours beneath the pines and hunt for crayfish in the murky shore waters. No one to disturb your morning swim in the nude.

There's pleasure in the city, too, where you can lie about all day in an apartment, reading, listening to records, ordering out for Chinese or Italian food. You can give each other backrubs with rosewater, and bathe in a tub of musk-scented oil. No need to go out at all—just eat and sleep and be together.

No matter where you set your love scene, your days and nights will blend in a happy fusion, with joyous lovemaking the center of your universe together. To assure that neither of you tires and withdraws from this happiest of pastimes, make the following aphrodisiac to be taken at least once a day:

Soft-boil three eggs, timing them at three minutes. When they're ready, add three tablespoons of molasses, and mix the eggs thoroughly with it. Now eat this food with grits (easy on the grits, you need all the room you can spare for the egg-molasses glop), and your strength for sweet pleasures will be assured for the whole day.

It's said that if you pull a mandrake from the earth without proper ceremony, its shriek of pain will break your heart and you will be cursed forever. But if you draw three circles around it with the tip of a willow wand, and tie a black thread from the plant to the collar of a white dog, or the yoke of an ox, you will be safe from its spell as the animal pulls it up. You will also own perhaps the most powerful herb in all of magic.

The mandrake is a literary herb, a cultured herb. Its pedigree is impeccable, and its cachet is huge—it's always found in the best magical circles. Shakespeare wrote of the mandrake, as did nearly every other great poet, and whole books have been devoted to analyzing its significance and influence in English literature.

The reason for all his mandrakemania, according to scholars on the subject, is that because it resembles man, it can be influenced by other-worldly spirits (especially bad ones). Any plant that has that kind of black power can be magically potent indeed.

If you're going to grow your own, be advised that, magically speaking, there are male and female mandrakes. It's the female you're after, as its root is forked and looks like a pair of human legs. The male, on the other hand, has a single root. You may wish to cultivate it anyway because, according to legend, if its leaves are chewed they produce visions, religious experiences, and other delights. Be careful of the mandrake root, whichever sex it is, however, as it's a magical plant and its misuse can cause an offender delirium, insanity, and a horrible death.

Deal properly with your female mandrake and it will prove to be an astonishing amulet (keeping all trouble from you) and a powerful aphrodisiac if you powder it and add a tiny particle to a cup of wine.

CHAPTER III

Divination

Is it possible, we wonder, that what appear to be random shifts of events in our lives and in the affairs of men are, in fact, not random shifts at all, but part of a related design in some grand, cosmic pattern? Ah, the theory of predestination. Those of us who stand firmly outside the influence of organized religion often avow that concepts of God and predestination are ridiculous, and that life has no meaning beyond the fact of its being. Life for life's sake. It evolved, simple as that.

But then you get into something like astrology, and realize that, yes, horoscopes are capable of predicting many of the events that occur in a lifetime. With surprising accuracy. So nonbelievers in predestination are left, like everybody else, wondering if they have all the answers after all.

All of humanity is involved in a giant guessing game about its origins. It's as if an unknown host has invited us all to his beautiful estate, the earth, and hasn't shown up yet to tell us who he is and why he's gathered us here. Who could this very rich and powerful host be? we wonder. Is he a voyeur, watching our antics on some hidden TV monitor for his own amusement? Has he forgotten he invited us, and we're just milling about here without any purpose? Or does he intend to come, apologize for being late, and explain the reason for his invitation?

Who can know? One thing we're all certain of, however: this party isn't all fun and games. People get killed, and some go crazy with fear and hunger. No one knows *what's* going to happen next, but the theorists among us are trying to find out. We've put computers to work making horoscopes. Among the spiritualists are mediums who can tell you that when you get home there will be two important letters waiting. And when you get home, there are two vital letters in the mailbox.

In the civilizations of the Fertile Crescent, there were born diviners who could read the entrails of animals and know what the future held. They believed that conditions on earth foretold the will of the gods in heaven. By reading the pattern of markings on a sheep's liver, for example, they could tell, moment by moment, if the gods were going to be kindly disposed to an enterprise. Nothing in the universe was a random event to them, not even the sounds a stomach makes (this divination was called gastromancy). Every happening to diviners was part of the natural design of the universe, and could be used to predict events in the future—because the future, too, is part of the design. Predestination. (There *could* be method to the madness of our host, but *who* and *where* is he?)

In Europe, later on, the gypsies and the peasants became adept at divining, and some of their methods can be traced to ancient techniques. Divining by water was used in all ancient civilizations of the Middle East (it is still used by Oriental peoples). The magician, even today, has his client ask his question about the future while looking deep into the water of a divining cup. Then he speaks his incantations, and a sign on the water's surface provides the answer (rather like reading tea leaves). We find as part of a Roman recipe for a love divination a modification of that technique in the instruction: if a maiden wishes to know if her husband will be wealthy, she should bathe in red wine and search the depths of her bath for a vision of a golden dawn.

The following methods of divining the future don't require the aid of a classical scholar, or sorcerer, or gypsy expert, although a few should be done in company with other witches. Most of the ceremonies are devoted to matters of the heart, as most witches I know are most interested in finding out who their husbands or lovers are going to be. (It would be depressing, anyway, to discover by divination that you, or your best friend, had only six months to live.)

Remember to keep your perceptions honed when divining, and be wary of rationalizing if you learn something you don't like. Should you be destined to marry an alcoholic or drug addict, and don't take firm measures to avoid meeting such men, you have only yourself to blame when you marry one.

✑ Acquiring the Gift ஓ✷

Not everyone, odd as it may seem, wants to know the secrets of his future. One friend of mine put it this way: "It's marvelous if you find out that wonderful things are going to happen for you. You'd get a tremendous psychological lift from knowing, for instance, that you were going to become rich, or that the book you've been writing will be published and you'll gain stardom on the Johnny Carson *Tonight* show.

"But supposing you discover that not only are you going to have financial troubles over the next few years, but that you've been wasting your time writing a book that will never be published. Isn't that going to influence you so that no matter how determined you become to make your book, say, beautifully written, something of your depression over the fruitlessness of writing it will show through and it won't be done well and therefore won't be published?"

It's very difficult to argue with this sort of well-made point. People vary in their reactions to bad news. It's certainly possible that learning your book won't make it could influence you to make the prophecy come true. But, on the other hand, other authors would work harder to overcome a supposed ill fate. My friend then asks, "So what's the point of learning what's in the future in the first place if the prediction does not necessarily hold true?"

My answer is that knowing what's in the future can aid you in choosing a course of action. If the prophecy says your book will fail, then if you continue writing it the way you have been, undoubtedly it won't sell. If you work to honestly evaluate its shortcomings, however, and take a new approach, then you've learned from the prophecy, and there's no reason why it shouldn't be overcome. Knowing what the future held in store has proved to be profitable and made you successful—you were served by the knowledge of imminent doom.

Divination, according to the ancients, is a technique that can be acquired. If you eat the tongues of seven adders, cut from their mouths when they're freshly slain, you'll learn the gift of prophecy. Shut your eyes and go to it!

◄§ Dreams of Divination §►

What sort of man will you choose for your husband? If you don't panic and marry the first man that asks you with whom you think you *could* be in love, it's likely that your instincts will guide you to a proper choice. Too often girls don't select husbands, but settle for them, believing, among other things, that by so doing they are being mature and realistic about love and marriage. What these girls don't realize, of course, is that being realistic about such totally emotional and unrealistic experiences as being in love and getting married is akin to the fruitless occupation of trying to fit square pegs into round holes. Realism and love do *not* go together. Strong first passions do fade a bit after marriage, but they're replaced by others equally strong, which defy analysis just as the heart-in-mouth variety do. So if a girl begins her married life with a vague fondness for her mate, but no strong loving emotion for him, what will her feelings metamorphose into later on?

All too often the answer is *nothing*. She feels nothing about him one way or another. If he asked her for a divorce, she'd probably give it to him—almost without a fuss. If she met a groovy man, she'd probably have an affair with him with no twinges save, perhaps, for a small one stemming from the Thou Shalt Not Commit Adultery commandment. No feelings, unfortunately, turn quickly into grudging ones —doing the dishes, the laundry, housework, and raising children grudgingly. Grudgingness, like stinginess, makes a woman mean and shrill, and everyone around her suffers for it.

Before you marry, be sure you love your man. Be certain that you have the feeling your mother always told you you'd have—"You'll know he's right for you when he comes along." It's a very real knowing, and you needn't fear that it will pass over your head unnoticed. To help you get some idea of what your man will look like, so you won't go off half-cocked and marry a blond when divination has told you he'll be a brunet, follow this ritual:

On St. Andrew's Eve, November 29, borrow a cup of water from a married neighbor and add a pinch of earth collected from the foot of an oak tree. Add two seeds from a pear, and when the midnight hour approaches, drink the mixture. Then go to sleep and your future husband will float through your dreams.

Are you afraid that you won't remember your divination dream after going to all the trouble of doing a ceremony before retiring? Although most of us can't recreate in the morning our every-night variety of dreams, rest assured that dreams of divination are vivid—almost like nightmares in their memorability—and that you'll have no trouble at all in recalling one.

Much scientific research is being done with dreams at the moment, and some of the most exciting experiments are being carried on at Maimonides Hospital in Brooklyn. At the dream laboratory there, scientists are trying to discover how often dreams are telepathically induced. In fact, it appears that a great percentage of them are; sleeping subjects do, regularly, pick up thoughts being projected to them by scientists.

Doing a divination ceremony before going to bed does expand one's general awareness and sensitivity. The ceremonies call for super-concentration, oriented toward the future by heavy thought and the paraphernalia of the ceremonies. Going to bed with your mind keyed for dream messages makes their appearance extremely likely. If telepathy works on a sleeping person, so do clairvoyance and precognition, which issue from the same wellspring of the mind. And precognition—knowing what will happen in the future—is what divination is all about. To meet your future husband in a dream, try this old French ceremony:

Draw a bath and add to it lemon verbena and hawthorn flowers. Soak in the bath and let the scents take over your being. Feel the odors permeating your body, your mind. Make your thoughts drift, as a tide, on the face of the world, seeing it pass beneath you from a height. When you're almost asleep, but still in this blissful trance-state, dry yourself, then rub rosewater on your breasts. Take yourself to bed and say:

Come my love, mon amour,
Fill my dreams with you.
Show me your face this night;
I give you me
When next we meet,
Be mine tonight.

One of the very best nights for a girl to discover who her future husband is to be, according to British tradition, is January 20—Saint Agnes's Eve. In its wee hours, English girls may be found doing eccentric things like crawling on hands and knees in moonlit, snowy fields, gathering winter grasses, or larking about nude in shadowy copses (though not for long on that cold night), singsonging rhymes of enchantment to inveigle the good saint to produce visions of their husbands-to-be. Candlelit kitchens, steamy with cauldrons of magic soups, are other scenes for the persuasion of Saint Agnes, and churches are filled on that eve with pretty girls beseeching her plaster image directly. On her special night, Saint Agnes, like Santa Claus, is one busy spirit, and it's a wonder she's able to extend her good offices to the number of anxious girls that she does.

Of course, the young diviners who know the best spells for catching Saint Agnes's attention are the first ones to have it. As in all magic, the ceremony is the medium through which the mind's concentrated power provokes action, so a time-tested, working ritual is more likely to help a witch confidently whip up the necessary pitch of power than one that, say, she makes up as she goes along.

If you wish to find out about your future mate, then follow this St. Agnes's Eve recipe which was told to me by a witch in London:

Boil a kettle of salted water and drop three garlic bulbs therein. Simmer the garlic for a half-hour, then remove it. Eat one clove from each of the garlics and take the remaining portions to your bed (better wrap the damp things in plastic wrap first). Now climb in, but before going to sleep speak these words:

> Dear St. Agnes, hear my plea
> Garlic keeps evil from thee,
> Visit me with a dream tonight
> Of my beloved husband-to-be.
> Dear St. Agnes, hear me.

Take yourself to bed, and wait for a visitation.

It may well be that you're not terribly interested in what your future husband will look like, but are, practically enough, perishing to discover what sort of career he will be engaged in. Are you going to wed a plumber? a sanitation engineer? a prizefighter? a millionaire playboy?

Since you're a witch, the range of positions your prospective husband could hold is limitless. You've no reason to feel trapped by a ghetto upbringing (be it Harlem or Palm Beach). If you're a poor witch, it's possible to select a bank president; if you're a rich witch, you can marry a colorful rock singer. Just anyone at all is within the realm of your possibilities, if you apply sorcery.

But to get a bead on what the future says it holds in the way of a husband for you at this moment (and rest assured that your immediate future changes and expands in proportion to what your head is letting you become), there's another old divination method that will help you find out. Naturally, since it's a very old technique, there's no provision for symbols to reveal whether or not he's going to be a real estate magnate or, for that matter, in one of thousands of other contemporary money-making businesses. Therefore, I have had to improvise a bit, and using common sense, interpret a few of the symbols for you as best I can (e.g., music undoubtedly stands for a pianist or a rock musician).

Go to a jeweler and buy a plain gold key. Put it on a gold chain, and, just before going to sleep, insert the key in your mouth. When you fall asleep and dream of wealth, you will marry a rich man; of a church, a minister; of a marketplace, a fruit vender; of a battle, a soldier; of flying, an airline pilot; of music, a groovy musician.

If you don't like the job that divination says your husband will have, you'd better get busy and work some witchcraft on your head to expand your possibilities and to elevate your goals.

Sometimes it seems as if everyone you know is suddenly getting married. Your best friend has just announced that instead of eloping, as she always vowed she would, she's going to have a *huge* wedding (ten bridesmaids) with an *enormous* reception at the great big social country club that everyones' parents, in your set, belong to. Oh, great. Just what you need. Naturally she's asked you to be maid of honor, and that means you're going to have to go through the whole ceremony and reception scene smiling!

And then you have invitations to two more weddings later on. Everyone but you will be settling down in the suburbs this year, and you haven't even got a prospect on the line. Of course, you could do a black ceremony and break up these happily affianced couples so you won't be left out, but that does seem a sour thing to do. Or you could announce that you've planned a round-the-world trip and won't be in the country to go to anybody's wedding—that would certainly make your engaged friends jealous and save you the torture of seeing them happily off on their honeymoons. You could also pack your bags, head for New York, find a job, and become a swinging single. Or, perhaps, a bitter single. Or worse, an addict or alcoholic in the East Village. It's all possible. But good grief . . .

The best thing to do, obviously, is to swallow the sharp-peaked lumps populating your throat, accept your fate (it's conceivable that it could be more exciting than a conventional life spent raising kids in suburbia), and attend your friends' weddings. Anyway, as maid of honor for your best friend, you will have a good shot at catching her bridal bouquet—especially if you bribe her.

You will also, by attending weddings, have the opportunity of collecting packages of wedding cake—the kind brides give out for guests to take home and sleep on. This always seems a rather odd custom to some people, but never to a single witch. She knows that these bits of cake have a distinguished history in divining magic. Peasant girls from many European countries have long been discovering who their husbands will be in one of several popular bridal cake ceremonies:

If you sleep on a piece of bridal cake (put it under your pillow), you will dream of your future husband. Or if you can get her to do it, have your mother (or a married friend) feed you half the cake from her fingers. Wrap the rest of it in a white silk cloth and put it under your pillow. You will dream, that night, of your husband to be. (I prefer the latter ceremony, as the vibrations are concentrated and intensified by the feeding technique.)

In matters of witchcraft, I am a loner. For working spells I much prefer the privacy of my own room, without company, to the ruins of some forgotten cemetery with a coven of friends. When working with other people, I find that distractions abound: Joann, for instance, looks uproariously funny to me in the nude, ecstatically grasping a gravestone and howling at the moon when she's engaged in calling down the devil to murder an enemy. The scene is too real, jogs my awareness awake, and I can't help exclaiming to myself, she can't be serious! At such unfortunate moments, the spell for me is broken, and I'm no use whatsoever to the groups' magical endeavor. In fact, I'm a drag. So I've learned not to go when the coven politely invites me to a Sabbat.

But I know that lots of people groove on the coven thing. One of my best friends, Suzette, says that her powers are only engaged fully at Sabbats, and she's able only then to direct her will with the precision of a laser beam. Since her will is such a powerful force, anyway, I sometimes wonder if she's subconsciously in the coven more for the social aspect. Suzette has always been the sort of witch who, in an almost offhand manner, could simply *wish* a broken leg on an enemy going off on a skiing trip and consistently have her revenge. She has one of the most powerful evil eyes I have ever encountered.

But for less gifted, or beginning, witches, group magic makes good sense. There is no question that several minds, projecting the same thought, are going to work a spell more easily than a single mind that, perhaps, hasn't been trained to amplify its powers to the proper pitch. Here is a fine group ceremony for divining who a future husband will be:

> With one or two friends, go, in silence, to a meadow and by the light of a full moon sit in a circle and light a fire of bay leaves in a silver dish. As the bay leaves flare, each of you must throw the flower of a marigold onto the flame. Still maintaining silence, return home and go to bed. Each of you will dream, during the night, of your husband-to-be.

One of the sad aspects of being married is that you can no longer look forward to the occasional love letter that once came your way. No more wisps of well-thumbed paper to tie up in lace ribbon and store on a closet shelf in a sacheted box. No more mooning over sentences that somersault your heart and leave your cheeks tingling. No more midnight hours to spend in puzzling over your own declarations when you should be getting your beauty sleep. And, sadness, no more soul-mate girlfriends to share his exulting lines with in sighs or giggles.

Favorite love letters are, somehow, forever committed to memory. Once, in a moment of complete frustration, just after I'd decided that marriage was obviously meant for other women but certainly not for me, I was surprised by my sudden recall of some sweet loving lines from another age. The particular letter I remembered was from a man who, at the very moment he wrote me his flowery declaration, was engaged to another girl. Remembering the pain accompanying the discovery of his falseness, and the vulnerability of being in love, my heart flooded with forgiveness and appreciation of my poor, long-suffering husband, and I spent the rest of the week apologizing for my silliness and evil temper.

If I had only known in those long-ago love letter days what I know now . . . For girls who find epistles in their mailboxes, and wish to discover if the writer means those words:

Put the love letter back in its envelope and quickly immerse it (after reading it, of course) in a solution of orris root and powdered myrrh with water. When it is dry, clip the word "love," wherever it appears, from the paper, and tear the avowals into the tiniest possible pieces. Mix the scraps well into whatever you're eating for your evening meal, and, as soon as possible after dinner, go to bed. If you dream of flowers, or anything having to do with nature (trees, oceans, the like), your lover means what he says: he loves you. If you dream of noises, people, or the night, he doesn't mean a thing he says at all. You're lucky that he's at the other end of pen and paper.

Late January through mid-March (when the weather finally starts warming up) is definitely the slump season. This is the time of year when all of your clothes suddenly strike you as hideously shapeless, everything you buy at the grocery store looks homogenized and tastes like cardboard, and all the men you see have complexions in the same shades as their dullest suits.

There seems little hope of getting all the way through the slump season gaily and gracefully, but if you plan a few sparkling activities, there can be some memorable bright spots. For instance, I'm all for taking the third week in February as a vacation and going someplace warm. The first two weeks of this horrid month can then be passed in anticipation, and there is time to go shopping for resort clothes even if you find after the air fare outlay that you can only afford a scarf.

Then there's the party you can finally get around to giving. March is marvelous for parties because everyone is just as bored as you are, and the excitement of a little festivity and the possibility of meeting someone new will assure you a full house. The trouble you go to will not then be in vain. Try mixing champagne and white wine and serving a variety of cakes, mints (perhaps homemade ones that are packed with magic aphrodisiac?), and strawberries with whipped cream. Have the party by candlelight and, if you have a terrace, put portable electric heaters on it so that pot smokers will be comfortable. You and everyone else will be greatly cheered by your effort.

The evening of January 21, however, should be spent by yourself, since this is Saint Agnes's night. Take two pins and two of your own hairs. Bind one hair about

each pin and lay these beneath your pillow. As you go
to sleep, whisper:

> Sweet St. Agnes, let me see
> My husband-to-be this night.

You will dream of the man you'll marry.

✥ *Divining by Materialization* ✥

If possible, beginning witches should ally themselves with
other new magic addicts. Being part of a group (not necessarily a full-fledged coven) gives a novice a chance to air her
magic philosophies and learn what others have to think
about sorcery. Also, members of a group are bound to exchange magical formulas, and quite a repertoire can be accumulated this way. (Since spells are not easy to come by in
authentic, unadulterated form, be certain always to check
the sources from which your friendly witches got them—
unwitting mistakes made during a ceremony can lead to
gargantuan backfires.) Also, groups, when meeting, usually
do exercises together to expand consciousness and promote
superconcentration. Later on, they work on projection, as
well, and may even accomplish, through witchcraft, some
group objective (perhaps getting enough money together to
take everyone to Haiti to study voodoo).

One group of advanced young witches I know about does
a lot of research and has a huge collection of esoteric spells
from such venerable occult sources as the Bibliothèque Arsé-
nal in Paris. They meet every Sunday night and, after coffee
and devil's food cake, gather around and perform one of
their fascinating ancient enchantments. Recently, they successfully accomplished the following divination to see their
future husbands:

Gather as many girls together as you might wish (although I recommend, personally, no more than thirteen) and as the moon rises go into a room which is entirely draped in white (bedsheets are ideal for draping purposes). Now all gather in a circle in the center of the room and join hands. In the center of your circle should be another one composed of white candles (one for each of you) which each of you has lit. Now, moving from right to left, all should chant the following spell:

> Circle of magic, chaste ring of white,
> Capture the face of my wedded love tonight.
> From the flame let him emerge,
> In the circle safe from harm,
> Subject to this magic charm,
> Round I go, round I go,
> Safe he'll be
> Let me him see.

Now, without breaking your circlet of arms, all sit in a tight ring and wait for the candles to produce the visions of your future husbands.

There's no one in the world more intent and single-minded than a girl bent on getting married. She can be just as militant and organized in her pursuit as the modern young woman who spends all of her energies staying single.

Marriage-minded ladies are to be found everywhere, but especially in large cities, where they tend to live in ghettos (every large city now has a singles district, packed with apartment houses that attract unwilling bachelorettes).

Girls in search of husbands tend to have lots of male friends—many of them discovered at singles bars—and jobs that don't collide with their social lives too much. While stewardesses appear to be always on the move, they say that this increases their chances of coming across the right man. Indeed, they're ubiquitous and competitive. Most of them get married within a few years of taking flight, and a high percentage snag rich husbands. (As wealthy men are notorious for regarding most earthbound girls they meet as pleasure bunnies, being airborne, it would appear, has a peculiar, heady effect on them. Perhaps Frank Sinatra said it all in the song "Come Fly with Me.")

Teachers, of course, have glorious summer vacations in which to husband-hunt, but as competition they're not in the same league with stews. Many of them spend valuable time looking for men in odd places. One friend of mine reports that a ship to Antarctica was S.R.O. with teachers, and another found her companions on an African safari not graying and wealthy males, but pretty young French teachers from Long Island.

Nurses, of course, headhunt among the doctors staffing hospitals and regard all other females who find doctors interesting, too, as intruders in their private preserves. They tend to be cliquey, snappish, and dangerous when competing for interns.

Now, all you dedicated huntresses, here are some divination techniques employed by Rumanian peasant girls who share your intense interest in discovering who the future husband might be:

> If you wish to know what your future mate will look like, go naked, just before dawn on Midsummer Day, June 24, to a quiet pond. Look for a perfectly round white pebble, and when you've found one, cast it in the water and speak these words as you throw it:
>
> > If I hear a bird cry, handsome he'll be.
> > If I hear the wind sigh, ugly to see.

Now listen carefully and learn your fate.

If you're modest, and find this method of divination somewhat indiscreet (I can't believe it), then get yourself invited to the seashore and try this method:

Collect three perfect shells from a beach and pound them together until they're dust. When the evening star appears, take a pinch of your powdered shells and scatter it on the tide. Then take another pinch and cast it in the sand. And take a third pinch and add it to wine and drink it. Before the moon fades, you'll dream of your husband-to-be.

If you're a believer in, and practicer of, true black magic (there's a lot more human sacrifice going on during magical rites in this country than anybody is really yet aware of), then Halloween night poses no celebratory problem to you. Obviously, you and your coven will meet to raise and praise the devil. If you're into classical sorcery, you're probably planning an important materialization for that night of one of the hierarchy of evil spirits to work some mischief for you.

But for us witches who prefer working our wishes with herbs and candles rather than magic daggers and fresh human hearts, Halloween can be a problem night. With no devil to worship, and no desire to cause anyone's death (if you do want someone dead, however, this is the night to hire yourself out as an assistant to your local classical sorcerer— he may be willing to slip your petition to the captive spirit he conjures), how can you, in a civilized way, take advantage of the powerful vibrations afoot that night?

Well, it is a perfect night for divination. It's the sort of evening when it's almost easy to materialize the face of a future husband, and have his image remain on view for a rather long time—often minutes, rather than the more usual seconds. Such ghosts from the future have even been known to speak on Halloween—a rare occurrence indeed—telling the conjuring witch when she may expect to meet and marry him (one of my witch friends was told by her vision that they would meet on a merry-go-round near New York City on July 12, 1969—they are, of course, now blissfully married).

If you wish to do some divination work on Halloween, here's a good, effective ceremony to perform:

> Sometime before midnight, place before a mirror an offering of wine and three hairs from your head. Now turn your back to the mirror and as the clock strikes twelve, listen for a movement. When you hear one, turn and look in the mirror. A vision of your future husband will greet you.

Some rituals of witchcraft are extremely risky to perform because if something should go wrong while you're doing them, the results could be disastrous—to you. It is easy to bewitch yourself accidentally. It's also usually true, however, that with high-risk ceremonies the rewards are great. If your witchcraft works, results are immediate and marvelous. To perform such important ceremonies, it is absolutely essential that you be a full-fledged adept. Beginners and intermediate witches should never fool around with recipes they're not entirely sure will come off.

The divination ceremony I'm about to describe is indeed a highly dangerous one to perform because the witchcraft involved crosses over the border from pure divination: You actually produce your husband. The witch who tries it should arm herself during the period of the operation with every amulet she can find, including a talisman with salt in it that she must carry or wear on her person at all times. Salt is the traditional means of keeping devils at bay, and in this ceremony the full panoply of devils must be barred from influencing the proceedings even minutely. (Be very careful, incidentally, never to spill even a grain of the salt from your talisman, as this automatically assures that a disaster will happen.) Here is the ceremony:

Just before midnight, one week before a full moon, put into a little silver casket (a silver box will do): yarrow, thyme, a snail shell, and a penny with a hole in it. Bury the casket just at midnight outside your front door, and set garlic in a circle around the spot. Each evening while the moon grows full, go to the spot where the casket is buried and say over it:

> When the moon stands full,
> Here he'll stand,
> My love forever more to be.

On the night when the moon is at its peak, dig up the casket, set it on your doorstep, and wait for your husband to come to you.

It's all very well to divine that you're actually going to marry someday, but doesn't the question lurk in your mind: "What in the world is my husband going to look like?"

"Could it be someone I already know," you ask, "and supposing, if it is, I really find him rather repulsive?" Ah, for a glimpse of the man, just to be sure he's what you have in mind.

The gypsies discovered a way to actually materialize a likeness of future husbands. It's a tricky ceremony, so you shouldn't choose it for your first attempt to divine the future. It also requires a visit to the country to perform, if you're an urban dweller, and not just any old piece of countryside at that. You're going to have to locate an area that has a bubbling brook. You'll also need to take with you a pail, an egg, dust from a well-traveled road, a needle and, if you're wise, some cotton and iodine.

Now sally forth on the night of St. George's Day (April 23), and proceed to the brook. Perform the following ritual on its bank:

With the pail, take water from the stream as it runs toward you. Now crack the egg, and let some blood from your left ring finger fall on it. Let the egg fall in the pail of water. Now, scattering the dust from the well-traveled road around you so it makes a whirling storm, cry, above the pail:

Come from the water, the dust, the blood, the egg of creation
A vision of my husband
Called up from the shades of future night.
Let me behold him, I say!

Stand very quietly, and watch as the form of your future husband rises slowly in the moonlight from the water in the pail, then slowly fades away. You'll have a few moments to glimpse his face. Whether you're happy or horror-struck over what you see, *do not forget* to return the water to the brook, or the spirits of the water will be angered. I have heard it said that they can cause death to a mortal who, after meddling with them, doesn't return them to the peace of their element.

◄§ Divining by Signs §►

It's all very well to conjure up a vision of your future husband, but supposing in the few seconds you had to glimpse his face, you forgot to notice if he was young or old?

Young girls do marry older men, you know, but if you have your heart set on a young, virile husband, by discovering his age you can take measures to protect yourself from meeting more mature types. (If you're at a party, say, and there's a group of them standing about being charming and attractive, leave early.)

Bear in mind, however, that older men are often more desirable as husbands than younger ones. They've usually been married before, so they know the ropes and they're consequently more understanding of your foibles—such as your inability to get within three feet of the stove without groaning. If you throw a tantrum, or a fit, the instinct of an older man is to be kindly and say "There, there" rather than take it all personally and slam the door on his grouchy way out to the nearest bar. Young husbands are often just as excitable as you are, but older ones have seen it all and usually remain calm.

The ritual to divine the age of a husband is not simple. It requires dedication to do, as there's a lot of footwork involved. It's also necessary to perform it in farm country:

Get fresh dung from a crossroads. Go for a hike and collect apples from three bountiful trees in different orchards. Get some water from six different spots. (This last ingredient requires ingenuity to collect and may take several days. You will probably have to visit various farmhouses and ask for drinks of water—carry a plastic bag with you, and surreptitiously spill some of the water into it.) When you have all your materials, delicately mix them together (slicing the apples helps). Now on St. George's morning, April 23, take your dung mess to a church, lay it in the road out front of it, retreat, and wait. If a child comes by and steps in the center of your patty, you're going to marry a young, beautiful man. If an adult walks on it first, your husband will be aged but wise.

New Year's Eve in northern climes is always one of the coldest nights of winter. It is also one of the best nights for divining who your future mate is going to be. Of course, if you live in California, this next ceremony should pose no problem: just take yourself to the nearest palm grove and proceed. But if you live in New York, bundle up in your warmest boots and furs and head for Central Park.

Straight from the gypsies, the ritual is marvelous to perform if you've got friends and, as always seems to happen, none of you has a New Year's Eve date. You can even make a little party of it. Invite your dateless chums over for leftover Christmas turkey hash, and a great deal of wine, and lots of loud, false laughter. Then all of you bundle up, fortify yourselves with flasks of brandy (pot's too dangerous to take, as parks, even in winter, are favorite fuzz haunts), and head for the trees.

When you reach a suitably quiet and secluded site (which involves hiking—see what I mean about dressing warmly and taking brandy for this one?), gather around a tree that still has a few dead leaves on it and do the following:

Form a circle, and dance about the trunk with your heads thrown back, looking at the sky. Chant the following incantation while doing that:

> Stars of the night,
> Bright stars of the night,
> Make the wind blow,
> Make the leaves fall,
> Who catches the leaves
> Will have her own.

If, during the course of the chant, a leaf should fall, whoever's nearest it at the time it tumbles down is in luck: she'll be married before the year is out. If nothing happens, though, she should renew the lease on her studio apartment.

Warning: if you and your friends were too high to be serious during the ceremony, cancel any hope that your group witchcraft will work. If a leaf falls, it's pure luck, not pure divination.

If you're single and living alone in your own apartment in a big city, there are times when the world closes in on you, and malevolently seems to want to suffocate you with its enormity. There it is, life in the streets, big and powerful, people doing things, busy, happy. Here you are, small, trapped within four walls, alone, and no one you want to see, with nothing to do, and destructively unhappy. If you have a mother or father you're close to, you probably call them up and bawl your head off about how awful it is to be alone. If you couldn't possibly consider calling them, you have a choice: go to bed and get a good long rest, or get yourself together and force yourself to call up a girl you know and invite her over for dinner.

If you are able to really cast off the weight of this heavy world from your shoulders and banish your black mood, there's a little divertissement that could bring laughs and smiles to your otherwise frowning face. Invite three or four girls over for a smoke or drinks or what have you, and when you're happily high, indulge yourselves in an amusing English witch game.

Go to the nearest park, and take with you wands made from the willow tree, and a ball of pink peonies, woven tightly together (your florist can probably oblige). Blindfold yourselves with silk scarves, and then you and your friends spread out, after placing the peony ball on the ground between you. Whichever girl first touches the ball with her wand and retrieves it will be the first married.

Of course, if you're not in the mood to find out that Susie, not you, is going to be the lucky one, and anyway you can't picture yourself and your friends in the park leaping around gaily attempting to locate a silly peony ball, you can always do the following:

Look fixedly at a waxing (or full) moon while binding your hair in a single braid, then go to bed and dream about the man you will marry.

There are a lot of important things you should be doing if you're single—much more important than sitting around twiddling your fingers, moping and groaning over when you're *ever* going to get married. If you're ambitious, there's no need for you to take some simple, going-nowhere job, just so you'll be ready to split the work scene when the right man comes along. But so many girls—including graduates of important women's colleges—are following this terribly down pattern these days. It's a trend. Perhaps a lot of girls don't feel the need to drop out of college, but they feel the need to, fashionably, drop out of the super-square, nine-to-five city job scene after school.

This means, obviously, a lot of freedom to do nothing much. A little money to do nothing much on. Instead of wasting living time working at jobs that require a lot of energy, and a large chunk of self, it seems more amenable to many girls to take life easy, enjoy relationships with people, and wait for that shadowy lover or husband who lurks just around the corner of time.

So what does that get you? I abhor the idea of working

just to make money—that's just as pointless as doing a nothing job to mark time. But to explore potential and brainpower in a good job is a very exciting trip. Suppose you've always wanted to write, wanted to say things and get your ideas to people, maybe influence them politically or artistically. You'll never write powerfully, influentially (unless you're the Barbra Streisand of the literary world) from a communal pad in the East Village where nobody works really hard at anything. It just won't happen. You've got to be where influential writing goes on, where there's electricity, where opportunities occur. Your mind's got to expand, to be educated in a disciplined fashion, and your skills have to be sharpened. If you're living the hip life, working halfheartedly, and spending brain cells wondering when you'll meet your man, forget about developing your potential. You'll always remain all talk and no action.

To help you get yourself together and over the where-is-my-one-true-love syndrome, so you can at least relax about it, here's a ritual to help divine when he's going to come along:

> Boil a small kettle of water. Just at noon, go outside with your kettle while it's still bubbling and put it where the sun glares on its surface. Now take nine almonds and, one by one, cast them into the pot from a distance of nine feet. As often as you put an almond in the pot, subtract one digit from nine. The resulting number is how many years it will be before you marry.

So your lover has been giving you a hard time, has he, rousting you about the blandness of the macrobiotic food you've been feeding him, snapping at you to improve your habits and clean the apartment once in a while. So what does he know? you ask. He hasn't even learned that you, like every other woman, are entitled to freedom of choice in the food you serve as long as you have to cook it, and to a neurotic habit or two. After all, he's a lover, not a husband, and if he doesn't like it, maybe he'd better move along.

Still, you're not sure. He's wonderfully kind in most ways, and fun to be with, and he does know how to handle your colorful personality quirks most of the time. Maybe he's right. Perhaps you should make the bed and vacuum the rug more often. And cooking meat and vegetables a couple of times a week for him wouldn't kill you. But at the same time, you wonder, what would Women's Lib advise?

So you decide that what to do depends on how much you value your singleness as opposed to how much you value having him around. How much store do you put in your complete freedom to do whatever in the world you like within the confines of your own apartment? Just how vital is it, anyway, that you can live in complete squalor if you want to? Well, squalor is awful, you concede, but you seem to have to have a need to be surrounded by it, or at least a need not to clean it up. Could you really bring yourself to do something about your horrible ways? Is this the man who can motivate you onward and upward? There's only one thing to do. Interrogate Fate and find out if you really want to handle all this hassling, nagging, and the bottle of furniture polish he presented you with this morning:

> Take a mirror out of its frame and write his name on the back. Now drop it on a stone (or tile) floor. If it doesn't shatter, prepare yourself for possible matrimony, and start cleaning the furniture.

Recently, I went with a friend to visit a marvelous psychic I happen to know in New York. No sooner was my friend settled in a comfortable armchair in this woman's apartment than the psychic stated, in a most straightforward and positive way, that my friend would be married within the year.

The woman passed over a deck of well-worn cards, which she told my friend to shuffle and cut into three separate packs "always toward you—never cut them away from yourself." She did this, and the psychic turned over the three piles and said, "There, I told you, it's right in front of you in the cards. You will be married within the year."

Stunned, my friend inquired who the man might be. She knew someone whom it had occurred to her she might marry, but the certainty that she would do so was far from her thoughts at that time. The psychic jumbled the cards together and told my friend to choose ten of them at random for her. Then she took the cards and placed them face up in neat rows and studied them intently. Slowly, she looked up. "It is someone that you know. Are you in love with anyone?"

"Well, sort of. I'm not sure, really."

"Well, it is someone you know. Look. This card tells me it is. If you see a man that interests you, get me the birthdate of this man and I'll tell you if he is the right one."

My friend thanked the woman, and we left. She was so puzzled over the prediction that I suggested she go home and try the following divination to learn more:

> Take round pellets of wax and write on each one the initials of a possible marriage partner. Now set the pellets, randomly, in a circle and with a needle (while you're blindfolded) spear one of the wax balls. Whomever it represents is your future mate.

Spring arrives when the air hangs sweet, and a first breath of it tugs at the heart, then wafts it skyward with heady joy and longing. This is no time to plod through the city streets to work or endure corroding smog; away to the country, the spirit begs, to frolic in a field or sit for hours by a quiet spring pond.

There are woods to be explored when the sun is high: crocus flowers unfurled in Easter egg colors, Jack-in-the-pulpits like tiny creches abloom in ivy beds, and violets on tender stems nodding perfume to the breeze. Tiny bugs begin their toils among the fresh grasses, and first locusts rattle awake in the high sunny trees.

There are spring streams to walk barefoot in, with polli-wogs swarming at the shore, and pussy willows in the rushes nodding sagely in the wind. Spring is for freedom, and lying beneath a blooming apple tree watching the blossoms float-ing pink and white in the sky. It's a fairyland of orchards, and parks of velvet grass, and no one should be left alone in the winter of the city.

Love is spring, and every heart should be seduced by it; there's no better moment for a love. You find daisies together and, childlike, pluck the petals to learn if your hearts are true. You give presents of woven flowers to each other, and kiss beneath arbors, and go for walks beneath the spring moon. The air tingles in your blood, and your fingers are light on his arm.

Will you find true love in the spring and marry? Go to a wood, close your eyes, and say:

> If I am to have a lover soon,
> Then spring beauties meet my gaze!
> If I am to marry someday nigh,
> Then violets let me find!
> If I'm an old maid to be,
> Then Jack-in-the-pulpit I'll see.

Whichever flower you see first when you open your eyes is the one that indicates your marital state.

From the earliest times, man has believed that the future is in some measure predetermined; by consulting it, he could choose auspicious moments to transact his affairs. The ancients sought omens from the gods to help them decide if the time was right for anything from making a purchase in the marketplace to setting sail to some distant land. In modern times, we speak a good deal of luck, which guides us to decisions either profitably or disastrously. And we often defer to our luck with superstitions—such as taking care in all matters on Friday the thirteenth. (How many apartment and office buildings, would you guess, lack a thirteenth floor?)

More and more frequently, our contemporaries are consulting horoscopes drawn up by adepts or computers (a $200,000,000-a-year business in this country). Astrology works on the assumption that one's future is predetermined (that is not to say, of course, that events predicted for our futures can't be redesigned by careful new action). So it would seem that a growing number of people are more able to accept a philosophy that includes the idea that one's actions are all predetermined, as opposed to a belief that we freely choose the actions that make or break us in the end. It is a short step to a now popular and growing belief in reincarnation. The idea that our conscious thought—call it soul, if you like—is constantly reborn (somewhat as raindrops fall, turn to moisture, and rise to become clouds and raindrops again) seems increasingly more consistent with Western theories of predestination. Interestingly enough, a scientist who for years has been studying people who are certain they have lived before has said that he would bet more for the probability of reincarnation than against it.

So divining the future is no longer quite the amusing pastime it once was, and students of the occult are becoming less scorned and more sought after for their talents. Chance doesn't seem quite so chancy any more, and luck is being looked into. If you, by chance, come across a single die, cast it and inform yourself on your next bit of luck:

> If one spot shows upwards, a visitor is coming. If two spots turn up, you'll have very bad luck. Three spots presage a pleasant day. Four spots, good luck. Five spots mean you may have an accident, so watch it. Six spots assure you'll have good fortune, and a lucky streak, if you're a gambler.

I don't ordinarily have much sympathy for girls who find themselves panicked, at the age of twenty or twenty-one, about whether or not they'll ever find a man and get married. Such girls, in the clutches of their fears, usually fall prey to all manner of unattractive behavioral quirks that are not only off-putting to the men they meet, but to women, as well.

Recently, I met a girl who impressed me as the archetypal frightened female. I was introduced to her at a party, and after a short, almost rude, hello, she re-engrossed herself in conversation with a man she had pinned (or so it appeared) against the wall. I filed her in my mind under people I don't want to know, and went on to meet other more fascinating guests.

Much later, I noticed that the man whom the girl had cornered was now talking to a relaxed, beautiful blonde standing near me, and that the clutched-up girl was nowhere to be seen. Needing more lipstick, I made my way to the bedroom for my purse; there on the bed was the missing girl, sitting stark-eyed and exhausted, with tears silently slipping down her cheeks. I couldn't retreat gracefully, so I asked her if there was anything I could do.

With that, she burst into uncontrollable hysterics, so severe that she wasn't able to speak for some time. I patted her shoulder and waited her out. Eventually, the girl told me that she was a complete wreck because every man she met rejected her almost upon meeting her. She was so upset about the phenomenon that not even the psychiatrist to whom she'd been going for six months had yet been able to exorcise these panic attacks. We talked for a while, and then I suggested that along with the psychiatry, perhaps she would like to try her hand at some witchcraft. I gave her the following two recipes, which, while they appear simple, are extremely effective when applied with proper concentration and projection:

> Hard-boil an egg. Hang it over the front door of your apartment with a sprig of bayberry, and the first eligible man to cross the threshold will marry you. Take a honeysuckle blossom and wear it in your glove. The first eligible man you shake hands with while wearing the glove will marry you.

I have a friend with very sharp eyes indeed, and she constantly exercies their quickness by keeping a lookout for interesting bits of refuse in the streets. Walking with her is a happening, an excursion of new dimensions. I have seen her nick from street gratings dollar bills that went unnoticed by hundreds of passersby, and cadge shiny hunks of glass for her fishbowl that seemed just dirty stones to me.

But what really fascinates my friend is ordinary nails, the kind carpenters use in two-by-fours. She says they're terribly expensive to buy in the quantities she uses them (her hobby is building floor-to-ceiling shelves for the giant collection of books she's accumulating) and that the city streets are littered with fine, straight ones. I've seen her collect as many as ten nails in one city block.

Since my friend is now into witchcraft, I've taught her to keep her eyes open for other objects, too. People lose the

most extraordinary things in streets: she recently picked up
a delicately carved stone that has the figure of Buddha on it.
She wears it as an amulet (naturally, we kept it around and
considered it for a while first, so that we could be sure it had
lucky vibrations).

What she looks for especially, however—and you should
keep an eye cocked for these, too—are tiny bits of colored
ribbon and string. If you come across a red ribbon, or red
stuff of any kind, on a walk, pick it up and wear it as an
amulet: you'll never have an enemy. (Be sure, as you pick
up the red string, or whatever, to say, "Red stuff keep trouble at bay; make my life sweeter each day.") If you should
come across some white object, or a white flower, look for a
letter with good news in it or expect to meet an influential
new man. A blue flower means you will have peace of mind
for seven days.

Like the Wandering Jew, gypsies roam the fields and for-
ests of Europe, gathering every spring in the French
Camargue to dance, sing, and feast, and worship the gypsy
saints. They have always been, and may always be, social
outcasts.

In Spain, after a bullfight, the gypsy women rush at de-
parting people, thrusting their babies into unfeeling, unsee-
ing faces; the babies wail, and their mothers cry, begging for
pesetas and, perhaps, for plain civil recognition. But the
faces of the crowd are blank, and the gypsies are pushed
aside, elbowed away, ignored, not even sneered at. Living in
caves, troglodytes, in the shadow of the Alhambra, or on
hillsides away from other human beings, the gypsies survive
and breed and steal to eat and work menacing spells against
those who torture them. In the midst of appalling poverty,
and the worst sort of evil discrimination, there is still time
for laughter, for dance, for hope and young love.

Since they first came from India in ancient times, the
gypsies have been the shadow people, the non-people. But

they never stayed in one place long enough to be physically enslaved; their gypsy freedom, however, is illusory. They're condemned to keep on the move, like the Wandering Jew, by hateful citizens.

But what of the hope and young love I spoke of? It can be found in the spells of gypsy maids, like this one from Ireland, to divine if a husband is in the near future:

> On Christmas Eve, as the clock strikes twelve, go outside and find three leaves in the high branches of three trees. Shake them down and, back inside, brew a tea with them. If a dog barks while you're drinking the tea, you'll be married within the year.

Men whom we would consider to be marriageable are, in some ways, harder and harder to come by these days. When I say "we," I mean those of us who are into witchcraft. A great many men, whom we might have fallen in love with once, are adding witchcraft to the list of things they laugh at and insult women about, and of course any man who would laugh at us is automatically ineligible.

As with so many other issues, people are becoming polarized in their views on magic. I've been dismissed as backward by too many once friendly acquaintances not to understand the frosty regard in which one polar group holds the supernatural. An artist I knew, until recently, all but exorcised me from a dinner party we were attending together for my presumptive belief that there might be other natural laws governing our existence beyond those that we currently understand. On the other hand, my companion at another dinner party sometime later was a Wall Street tycoon who not only understood my thinking, but intuitively grasped magical concepts that I lightly passed over, not wishing to monopolize the conversation and bore the other dinner guests. Those people who can understand magic fall into no neat categories, and the likeliest-looking curly-mopped art director may be just the man who finds sorcery medieval.

Try to stay away from men who out of hand reject magic, because they'll not only be hostile to you (and therefore unmarriageable) but, I think you'll find as I have, they suffer from brain atrophy on many levels. They're the I-have-to-see-it-before-I'll-believe-it people. So be careful when using the next divination technique to discover your husband, and place yourself where the most likely sympathetic candidates should be:

Light one white candle and one red one on each of seven nights, placing them in your window (use fresh candles each evening). On the morning of the eighth day, the first eligible man you encounter will marry you.

Perhaps more than New Year's, Christmas is a holiday that cannot be spent alone. To do so is to invite an orgy of self-pity with accompanying waves of depression that can drown all hope of your ever having a happy moment again. Christmas depressions are among the worst; the malaise that most people feel at that season can, in more serious forms, cause others to commit suicide. This does seem extreme, but if you've ever watched fairly healthy friends with no plans for Christmas Day scurry around trying to drum up *anybody* to invite them over for Christmas dinner, you can see that a seriously depressed person might go round the bend under the strain of having no one to be with.

Should you have to spend the holidays away from your family, plan far in advance some diversions that will keep you very busy. If you don't know of any parties you can get yourself invited to (although this is unlikely, as the Christmas party grapevine is undoubtedly the most efficient of the year), then give one of your own. Send out invitations early,

and from the RSVPs you'll be able to discover who's planning to be around when that wretched day arrives. Then you
can find out who might like to go skating with you on
Christmas afternoon, who might be dying to see a new
movie with you on Christmas night, and, most important,
who is serving Christmas dinner for stranded friends. As you
see, the secret to the season is to keep on the move.

But late at night on Christmas Eve, you may be faced
with some emotionally depressing moments. This is when
your memory drifts back to childhood and thoughts of Santa
Claus and Christmas stockings hung by the fireplace. This is
also when you should plan a magical divination ceremony
to distract you and raise your spirits. A witch friend of mine
says the following technique is her favorite for that night:

> Put a piece of coal, a spray of holly, and a pine cone
> under your pillow. Go to sleep, and before dawn your
> husband-to-be will visit you in a dream. In the morn-
> ing you'll see him walk beneath your window. (Don't
> run out after him, however, or you won't marry
> him.)

Once you've been into witchcraft for a while, chances are
you'll discover, as many witches do, that you'll never be
happy as an ordinary sort of woman—the kind who marries a
regular guy who becomes regional sales manager for the
insurance company. You'll probably find that the idea of
playing bridge on Tuesday afternoons with some friends
really bores you to death, and that belonging to a country
club is beyond your pale.

Ladies who practice witchcraft are, as a group, unconven-
tional, and their life styles, married or unmarried, tend to be
colorful. There's a solid, independent streak in witches that
makes it difficult for them to settle down and do the housework when they could be out collecting spells to turn up

money for a trip around the world, or hexing city administrators who drag their feet on such issues as air pollution and poverty.

Witches are incapable, too, of having stodgy husbands who think wives should be ornaments. Ornaments do frivolous things, and witchcraft is hardly such a pastime. A witch who accidentally marries such an old-school man usually becomes hostile to him in the end—a dangerous state of affairs. Scorned women act, and scorned witches, without second thoughts, cast black spells on erring husbands.

To avoid stodgy men, stay away from stodgy habitats. Don't take a job, as a rule, on Wall Street or Madison Avenue in New York, and don't live in small towns, especially in the Midwest and South. Live in the lively parts of large cities, and don't regularly hang out at singles bars that attract old-fashioned young lawyers, brokers, and I.B.M. types. Find out where *your* sort of man hangs out (cool guys hang about together, just as the stodgy ones do).

When you've surrounded yourself with a reasonably enlightened circle of friends, wait for Saint Valentine's Day, then divine when you will marry your up-to-date man:

Go out of the house early on St. Valentine's Day. If the first animal you see is a white dog, you will be married within seven months. If you first see a black cat, you may never marry.

There are a number of situations that spell automatic doom in a marriage, and one of the most obvious and most important ones has to do with money—the lack of it. It's absolutely essential to discover before you marry whether you're the sort of woman who needs money and the security it brings. You find this out by being completely honest and forthright with yourself about it. Money is not something dirty, something to be abhorred. But if you've gotten ·urself into a bag where you're convinced that you're above money—when, in fact, you have a need for it—then watch out if you marry a man of modest means.

For example, I know a girl who believed she didn't need money, and she's been married to a rather poor guy for thirteen years. But every moment of those thirteen years has been sheer hell for her, and she's a snappish monster whose very fingertips (which twiddle often) betray her unmitigated frustration. I suspect that because she's not too attractive, she's afraid of divorcing her husband. She probably thinks she'd never marry again—not attractive enough to catch another man. But if she'd only think of the ruin she wreaks around her . . .

Here is a divination ceremony to discover what profession your future husband will have. If it doesn't suit you, you had better take steps to travel in more rarefied, moneyed circles:

Take a deck of cards and shuffle it well. Now turn the cards up and watch for any of the following ones (whatever turns up first indicates your husband's profession):

Ace of hearts, a clergyman; ace of spades, a thief; ace of clubs, a lazy good-for-nothing; ace of diamonds, a millionaire; king of hearts, a philosopher; king of spades, a gambler; king of clubs, an artist; king of diamonds, a white-collar worker; jack of hearts, a professor; jack of spades, a cad playboy; jack of clubs, a daydreamer; jack of diamonds, a drudge.

CHAPTER IV

A Few Spells for Men

My first emotional reaction about the idea of including this next chapter was entirely negative. I felt, as I'm sure
you must, that it's a bit of a dangerous intruder. Here I've
been arming us women with powers that can put men just
exactly where we want them—under our spell, subject to
our will—and now I'm about to enlighten men so that they
can have the very same power over *us!* But I've carefully
thought about it, and I think I should help men out a bit, too
(in a very small chapter, please note, and *only* on the subject
of love—there are no spells to injure enemies, possibly meaning you, here).

It's easy to regard men as either love or hate objects—the
key word being objects. But men are living, breathing
human beings, not really the images we conjure up of them
and concentrate on in our minds. They're people with honest
feelings and emotions, not the potentially dangerous two-
dimensional creatures we may sometimes make of them.
Men are not necessarily out to completely do us in, as it
sometimes appears, but are just as capable of handling
magic wisely, and with good, not evil, intent.

On further reflection, it's not at all unflattering or unpleasant to think that an attractive man may wish to ensnare us with a love spell. And that's another reason that I wanted to include this chapter. Supposing that a divine man was coming to dinner, and this book was on an end table, and after a while you found him thumbing through it and pausing over the section on love magic for men. If he takes out paper and makes some surreptitious notes while you're in the kitchen seeing to coffee, can't you imagine how glowy you'd feel knowing that he probably wants to bewitch you?

The catch, of course, is that an equally unattractive man can just as easily happen upon your spellbook and enchant you. My advice, therefore, is to keep your book in a private place, and bring it out only when you have a special man you want to happen upon it. It's up to you to treat your book of spells with the same care and respect with which you work your magic.

There's another catch to this chapter that I've built in as further protection against the misuse that some men might contemplate putting these love spells to. Most of the magic is of a rather advanced nature, and while a seriously interested, clever man with some practice can make them work, less adept souls can run into some horrendous troubles. Boomeranging love magic has such effects as turning every woman the magician meets into a pillar of scorn. And, of course, there are no such happy moments as dates with pretty girls for the sorcerer who has erred. Pretty girls run, horrified, at the thought of an evening spent with him.

A few of the love spells are for beginners, so I'm not altogether casting the odds in favor of the lady witches. The trick is to practice with the easier ones—misfires are likely to be less devastating. Once you've mastered your modest goals with the easier love spells, then move on to the more important ones that will enable you to form more permanent liaisons, or win wives.

Always bear in mind that the key to magic is the ability to conjure in the mind's eye perfect images of the person desired (practice summoning visions of friends, of familiar surroundings, to sharpen this ability). It is also necessary to be able to work up huge emotion and project it at the person you desire, using your mind's image as the focal point. Spells help you summon your powers, help you concentrate, help you focus your thought and project your will.

Stunningly beautiful girls, the old saw goes, are often to be found at home, by the telephone, because none of the men they meet imagine for a second that such gorgeous creatures could actually be without equally gorgeous male companions. All the time. But as is not usually the case with old saws, this one really holds true. Really spectacular women do have trouble finding men to take them on even so simple an excursion as a trip to the beach. (Do you suppose beautiful blondes are often dumb because they never get taken out for a walk or to a movie and have no opportunity to learn anything?)

One really great-looking girl I know does go out occasionally, but complains of hangups that wouldn't immediately occur to most men (or to women, who, by the way, can be ferociously snotty when gossiping about a beautiful girl whom they imagine to be distant or even a bit stand-offish). It turns out that most men, in the company of melting beauty, see only the beauty and not the woman behind the face and body. The beautiful girl is often regarded as an object with no personhood, and, of course, she senses this and is hurt. Such girls learn how to deal with their hurt early, and sometimes retreat, distantly and permanently, into protective shells. Or they grow up to be painfully shy. And some girls, for one reason or another, get the idea that being beautiful is somehow sinful, and they go around feeling guilty about their faces and bodies.

Whatever the aberration, there are few truly beautiful

women who trust the motives of men, and they spend most of their time wondering if they're being courted for their minds or just for their bodies. If you happen to know a really lovely girl who turns you on because she's more than a pretty face, try the following love spell on her (a good one for beginners) and see if you can win her heart.

Take a potato and put it in a glass container with lots of fresh water. As you do this, vow undying love for your girl. Every day, check it for new growth, and as you do this say:

> May my love come to me,
> As the spirits of the water
> Bring life
> To this root.

Be sure to conjure your beauty's image perfectly in your mind's eye as you put the potato in the water, and as you speak your daily incantation over it.

You met her one June evening at a party on the beach, when the air was still and sweet, and the waves soft whispers on the sand. She came and sat near you by the fire, and the flames sparked light on her face and drew gold waves in her hair. You were unable to speak, and stared and time stopped.

When you finally came to, she was smiling at you, and you moved closer to her, and fell in love with her voice and her smile and her softness in the firelight, and you kept wanting to pull her apart from the others and walk alone with her in the moonlight and kiss her.

Finally, all these things happened. And you weren't sure if she was real, or some spirit sent to bewitch you, or your own imagination run mad and this beautiful woman a creature of

it. But then you were sure she was alive and breathing and
even looking very much in love with you, too. She quickly
said yes when you asked if she'd like to go for a long drive in
the country next day.

You never before had succumbed to love at first sight, but
that June night you gave yourself over to pure passion; and
in the weeks that followed, you realized just how much of
your self was out of your hands and vulnerable. Love was
deepening, your heart complete. If she left you now, you'd
be completely lost, a ship cut loose from its safe mooring.
But your love prevailed, and your emotions, tuned to the sun
and moon and the limitless expanse of the earth's beauties,
couldn't be checked, and you rose free of caution and embraced the whole of life; you were hers.

This total freedom from the walls of self-preservation that
protect the heart could be your undoing. Such great passion
often ends in great pain. But there is an English charm to
protect you if you've gone so far to sea there's no returning:

Put a leaf from a tree (preferably ash) in your
mouth, and turning to the sun, speak the following:

> Sun of heat, Sun of light,
> Bind my lover's heart tight.
> Never let her run from me,
> So our love will ever be.

Then take the ash leaf and cut it into thirteen pieces
and add it to food that your love will eat. If she swal-
lows just one section of the leaf, she'll be moved to true-
hearted love as complete as yours.

There isn't a woman alive who doesn't grow up dreaming
she'll marry Prince Charming. Oh, he wears groovy clothes
—jumpsuits, velvet jeans—in her mind's eye these days, but
nevertheless he's Prince Charming. He could be an artist or

an Establishment tycoon, but for all women, through every moment in history, his eyes are dreamy, his smile divine, his kisses soul kisses that make her quiver.

This imaginary man comes calling and always brings flowers—perhaps a rose or some forget-me-nots and violets. He's gentle. He's utterly gallant and respectful. (If she says something silly or ignorant, he glosses it over, then corrects her kindly. If she's in a truly chic restaurant and drops her wineglass, full, on the floor, he's on her side and makes the accident seem an act of fate, or maybe the glass's fault.)

When he makes love to her, he's hers. He's not thinking of the other ninety-nine possibly more ugly, possibly more beautiful, girls he's known in the last year. If she's frightened, he takes the time to talk to her between kisses and reveals himself—his passion for her, his caring—until she's sure that their loving matters to him. Then he's happy for her and for himself.

This man, in a word, is romantic. He's real and he's warm and human. He's not the taker who regards his lady as a cocktail conquest. He's the man who affirms life and humanity, and his woman as a feeling being—not the chiffon fantasy of a voyeuristic dream.

Sadly, there are so few romantic men. They aren't, truly, flower children or Italian lovers or Frenchmen in Paris or idealistic revolutionaries. They're rare lovers who fall in love and go to the ends of the earth to nourish that love. They are the superb men who might cast this spell:

> Steal an earring from the girl you love. Place it in a little bag of blue velvet with some hair from your upper lip and a morning glory bloom. Wear the bag about your neck, and she'll come be your love immediately.

From the kind of letters that the "Playboy Advisor" column receives, not every man in the world is having the easiest time of it, seducing every woman that attracts him. "We've been going together for two years, and every time I begin to get passionate with her, she removes my hands and says she wants to be a virgin when she marries." *Playboy* usually has something to say like "You've really got a problem on your hands; why don't you start going out with other girls?"

Of course, such advice stems from the presumption that all the man wants from his girl is a little physical involvement; there's no consideration of the larger frustrating situation, which is probably that the guy's *in love* with the girl. He's stuck with loving someone who isn't modern and can't accept the idea that if you're mad about a guy you *can* make love with him. (Old-fashioned ladies don't really understand that God doesn't send down punishing lightning bolts, or that warts don't suddenly start growing all over the body, because they've had sex.)

If you're in love with someone, and have tried *everything* to get her to give in—with no success—then try this magical ceremony to arouse overwhelming passion in her. She'll learn what "yes" means in a hurry:

Construct a figure of a girl in wax with the bosoms clearly made. The lips should look as much like your girl's as possible. Across the breast of the doll write her name, and on the back draw a circle with a five-pointed star in the middle of it. Then say over it:

> Rise her passion, rise for me,
> Let her heart engulfed be,
> Make [her name] submit to me.

Now take the figure and carefully insert a needle in its heart. When you go to bed, take it with you and lay it next to your face on the pillow. In the morning, wash it in water, doing so once in the name of the Father, once in the name of the Son, and once in the name of the Holy Ghost. Then douse it in rosewater and set it outside to dry in the sun. When you want to stimulate your love's desire, take your doll in both hands and project enormous passion at it. She will be completely uninhibited in your arms when next you meet.

One of the most magnificent attributes that men possess is an almost limitless lustful appetite. Pure, unadulterated sex for you. Faced with a gorgeous woman, you don't hang back coyly, viewing her bounties with reserve and from afar; you turn on and plunge right in, eyes alight and every gland in your body alert with desire. The come-on is marvelously aggressive, the fulfillment uninhibited. And once your lust is satisfied, it's only a matter of minutes before you're ready to be titillated again.

Women, on the other hand, hang back ("Is it me he wants, or my body?") and make a nuisance of themselves with their "I'm *not* like that" responses and generally slithery ways. (The few ladies who are behaving as they please when it pleases them, meanwhile, are having a marvelous time.) It's not so grand to be a strait-laced girl, restricted by guilt and the horrendous inner arguments that go on about kissing—then, what next, gracious, sensual fingering, then, what next, good grief! And while it would be perfect if women could step beyond their madonna-ridden, nunlike conscience nightmares and affirm themselves and their rights to pleasure (so how come men aren't warned from birth they'll go to hell for philandering?), this isn't the case, is it?

Silly you, you've fallen for an Afro-haired slinky beauty and, what else is new, she's a malingerer. What you must do is bring out the hoyden in her, and here's how to do it:

At the earliest opportunity, lend your woman one of your handkerchiefs. When you've retrieved it, used, wrap in it the Oriental root, ginseng. Now put fresh coal in a brazier (a hibachi is fine if you can't locate a brazier), and burn the root and hanky together. While you do this say:

> Let [her name] lust for me as
> This flame grows higher.

Concentrate on her face as you speak your spell, and she'll be yours before the moon turns.

Having the ability to go around casting spells on whomever one desires is entirely fabulous. But, as with most power, a measure of responsibility goes along with it. Any power that's used injudiciously, haphazardly, and without careful thought eventually snarls back around the user and trips him up. When we upset the balance of nature, we pay for it; and when we use power incontinently, we pay for it. The natural state of the universe is harmony—discord is, inevitably, rejected. If we cause disorder with misused power, we become vulnerable to all manner of terrible repercussions.

I have a friend, a gorgeous young magician, blue-eyed and golden-haired, who, for some reason, became obsessed with the idea of making every desirable woman he met his slave. He could have done this without even trying (let alone using magic), as there aren't too many mortals walking around endowed with the face and body of Apollo. Nonetheless, his obsession caused him to use the spell I give you next on perhaps fifty girls. Each one groveled at his feet. His apartment rocked with women. One girl did nothing but polish his shoes. Another spent hours ironing his socks. A battery of girls in the kitchen produced delicacies by the hundreds, until he was surfeited. Others bathed him and oiled his body and tended him until he grew limp with attention.

It was just at this point that he met a dark-haired woman; it was desire at first sight, and nothing would do but that she, too, must fall under his spell. He practiced his magic, and she came to him that evening. He was on the verge of making love with her when she began to chant; in a frenzy she rose up and hurled curses at him and called down the princes of Satan to destroy him. She was a witch; he was undone.

The spell broken, his slave women, released from his power, circled him, cursing him, tearing at him with long fingernails, while my friend lay on his bed unable to protect himself. Their violence grew; I arrived just as a frenzied blonde lunged at his throat. Immediately, I threw myself on her and tore her away. Everyone froze. I shrieked an enchantment; one by one they left.

My friend has never been the same. He's lost his zest for life. When he does manage to want something, it's a product of his jaded appetites. He does very little but lie in bed. A kindly girl looks in on him every day and sees that he eats something, but he's burned out, incapable of functioning. Eventually I hope to get him to a psychiatrist to see if something can't be done for him.

When you use this next spell, be very certain that you know what you're doing. If you've never practiced magic, don't experiment on this one first. Novices aren't adept enough to make women their slaves; if the spell should backfire, it could kill you.

Take a piece of fresh parchment and on it draw three concentric circles. In the center of the circles write the

name of the woman you desire with a quill pen dipped
in ashes. Now prick your left thumb with a needle, and
using the blood therefrom, draw, within the ring closest
to her name, seven five-pointed stars, at points equidistant from each other. In the next ring draw (in blood)
seven open eyes, with the pupils sketched in, also at
equidistant points, and in the outermost ring, seven
quarter moons (in blood) with the points facing
west.

Now fold the parchment in half, then in half again,
and go outdoors with it. Take with you a black candle
and a horsehoe made of iron. When you're in a private
place (a garden, a meadow, wherever), put the candle
on the ground and light it. Now, kneel before the candle and, holding the horseshoe toward the moon with
your left hand, burn the parchment in the candle flame.
While doing this, cry out the following incantation:

> Lord of the Night, of the Moon, the Stars,
> All-seeing Eye,
> Hear me.
> Great Lucifer, Beazelbuth,
> And all the fallen angels of the realm,
> Hear me.
> I command that you come here to this place
> And listen to me.
> Get this woman [say her name]
> And bring her to me,
> Drive her to me,
> Take her soul and give it to me.
> Lord of the Night, Great Lucifer,
> Do as I command
> Or I will curse you with angels
> And the eternal light of Heaven.

Now repeat the incantation, then take some of the ashes from the burned parchment, and with them draw a cross over your heart. Bury the horseshoe and the candle where you knelt and, visualizing her face, go home and to bed. Within two days, your woman will come, your captive, unto you.

Occasionally a statistic will shock me. I don't usually put much faith in them, but recently I read that between thirty-five and forty percent of all married women apparently have committed adultery. What's shocking about this statistic is that I don't see how you can fiddle around with it, as you can with most such figures. Either thirty-five to forty percent of all married women have committed adultery or they haven't: it's that cut and dried. (The figures on male cheating are something else again, of course.)

What such a statistic indicates to me is something I've believed for some time. Marriage is dead. As we know it, anyway. With all those unhappily married ladies running around, and the feminist movement gaining a head of steam, it won't be long now until we will all be hearing eulogies on the death of the American wedding. Naturally, the prospect is marvelous, because it means that by killing off marriage as we know it, we will have had to face the miseries that plague the institution and come up with a new and better system. Marriage is a relationship. We all need relationships. What we need is a better form within which to express our relationships. I'm currently voting for a marriage license that comes up for renewal every year or two. (Ideally, of course, I'm for free love, but that's generations away in our culture, where religious influences will continue to make this idea a no-no for some time.)

If you are appalled by a currently unhappy love affair (be you married or otherwise) and no longer can stand your self-enforced state of monkhood, you will be happy to learn that there is an eighteenth-century French magical formula to give you instant success with any woman you want for a lustful fling.

Approach your lust object and touch any part of her that's handy. While doing this, chant:

> Touch of lust,
> Turn to me,
> Your body to mine,
> Your lust to me,
> Make you mine.

It always amuses me when I unearth a man who, professing his modernity, is, in fact, wrapped head to toe in the neat transparent bag of Victorian morality. Confronted with a truly contemporary female whose mind is in the rarefied realm of making love relationships work now as all such relationships will probably work in the future, our modern man begins to wriggle and squirm in his Victorian bonds. "But, but, but," stumble his phrases.

Mother's place is no longer in the home ("but, but, but"), marriage has no validity any more ("but, but, but"), the exploitation of the female body must go—no more topless waitresses, down with *Playboy* ("but, but, but"). There aren't more female artists because oppressed woman suffers from dishpan and diaper mentality ("but, but, but").

The truth is, the consciousness of women is expanding at about triple the rate of the awareness of men, and herein lies a peculiar problem: men don't really know how to cope with girls who are thinking into the twenty-first century. Men are intrigued by contemporary girls, but they're having a hard time relating to them. They're a bit afraid of getting involved, too, because a guy would really never know, would he, what to expect next from a liberated wife—"Down with babies"? "Down with *sex*"?

But if you think you'd like to take on a modern woman (alas, if you don't in the end, as all the best girls are entirely with it), then try this old Czechoslovakian love spell to attract her attention (if you become really good at this one, she may capitulate and marry you!):

> Get five chestnuts (you may buy them if you like) and when you get them home, take a single piece of red string and bind them to each other, knotting the string three times between each nut. As you tie each knot, repeat the following spell:

> > I make this knot to
> > Snare the heart of
> > [Speak her name].
> > Let her neither sleep nor rest
> > Till she turns to me.

Another one of the great sadnesses that come of being married or living with someone for a long time is loss of the fantasy, or the state of self-hypnosis, that we usually call "being in love." It's altogether marvelous to *love* someone—to feel gentle and protective toward her, to adore the qualities that make her a unique human being, to know, soul-deep, that whatever happens, she cares about you, cares what happens to you, and you feel the same way for her. But for romantics, loving someone isn't always enough. Without the sensation of being *in* love, some people begin to wither, feeling they're losing a part of themselves, and afraid that their emotions—all their senses—are atrophying.

Being in love lubricates the feelings and awakens parts of the mind and body that usually lie dormant. Without emotional vibrancy, without a complete sense of aliveness, the poet in us falls asleep and we feel poor, neutered. Artists simply cannot write or sculpt or photograph brilliantly without being fully alive and aware; insights don't spring from fallow emotions. Where there is no feeling in an artist, there is no integrity to his art, and we can sense that. Not only is there lack of feeling in the work, but what we gather is a lack of the artist's caring that turns us off.

Sometimes it is necessary for two people who love each other to part and restore the parched bits of themselves with the fantasy, the illusion, of love—by falling in love. When you really love someone, there are few mysteries about that person to grasp and use to fall in love all over again. Oh, these subtle depths and nuances of course exist in a loved one, but the tortuous road to their discovery can be too much for a man whose thirsty need for immediate feeling is as great as a desert traveler's for water. To help satiate that need for quick, emotional fulfillment, here is an old Italian love charm that will quickly bring you a lover, a spring shower for your wilted spirit:

Give a chosen girl a drink in which you've let two tears (one from each eye) fall.

It's truly refreshing for a woman to discover that the man she's married to is actually jealous if another man, any man at all, pays the slightest attention to her. A husband who, bearlike, gruffles and snuffles and scares off would-be pursuers makes a girl feel truly wanted and important and puffs up her sense of security about the marriage. Jealousy in a man is something a woman can see and trust, far more than a thousand avowals of love that he might make to her. Love avowals, even from husbands, have a way of dissipating with the first glints of morning sunlight. Jealousy blooms in the day with people about.

There is nothing, however, so off-putting as a husband who is overly jealous. If you query your wife about her daily doings with more than simple, loving interest in her comings and goings, she's going to sense, after a while, that you're grilling her. And she's naturally going to resent it. She may even, at some point, throw in a little innuendo about some man she met, then drift on to other matters—just to test your reactions. If you ask, "How well do you know So-and-So?" or "Did he take you for a drink?" or some other stupid question, she may become angry enough to lie and say, "He used to be my boyfriend" or "He's taken me for drinks twice now." Thus, if you insist on letting your jealousy invade your wife's privacy, watch your nose when she slams the door in your face.

If you know that you are an extremely possessive man and are probably losing your wife's interest because of it, then what you had better do is use the following love charm recommended in an eighteenth-century book of spells.

To keep your wife lustful and interested only in you, let nine drippings from a candle of black wax fall into a glass of red wine. As you do this say:

> If ever [speak her name]
> Strays from me,
> Let her burn with Hellish fire.

Now get your wife to drink your potion, and all will be well.

Jealousy is really one of the more hopeless emotions human beings are subject to, as once it gets a leechlike hold, neither salt nor fire nor sheer determination will shrivel or loosen its grip. There it lies, a sickly slug coiled about the heart, slowing and smothering the beats till all good sense is gone. Then fear and rage take over, compulsively guiding the heart to disaster.

One girl I know well married an exceedingly rich man who loves her blindly. When they were first married, he bought her every conceivable gift, and they traveled everywhere together (including three trips around the world) in considerable luxury and in rarefied company. When they visited India they stayed with the Maharajah of Jaipur, and when they went to Java they lived in a nobleman's palace. And as his wife is a beautiful girl, this wealthy man gradually became jealous of the attentions lavished on her by their famous and mighty hosts. They stopped traveling and settled down in an enormous townhouse in New York.

My friend is a most marvelous hostess, and once her home was sumptuously decorated, she began giving parties and easily moved into the busy social life of New York's wealthy residents. Her husband, however, was permanently injured by his jealousy, and took to following her on her daily rounds. His black limousine would slide up to the hairdresser's where she kept an appointment every morning, then follow her to the restaurant where she always planned lunch with some lady friends. In the afternoon, it would move slowly past the boutiques where my friend shopped for her wardrobe of amusing evening clothes. Strangely, my friend never mentioned her husband's incessant checkups, and I'm not sure that she ever really knew about them, although I easily spotted his car whenever I went with her anywhere.

One night I had the opportunity to get into a conversation with my friend's husband about his perverse jealous condition, and I recommended a fidelity test to him that I felt might ease him somewhat. He's used it ever since, and has even been able to discontinue his compulsive following (he only checks up occasionally now). From a marvelously talented male witch who lives in New York, the technique goes:

Buy a garnet and have it made into a lavaliere. Give it to your wife, and watch it carefully. If she's ever unfaithful to you, it will change color.

It seems to me that, by now, you have been warned enough about the dangers of fooling around with sorcery. I hope you have heeded my words. But I know that some of you are, inevitably, the sort of men who live precariously. When you go skiing for the first time, you go to the top of the highest mountain, whip out your beginner's manual, and start down. When you drive, you always drive fast—especially when you're high.

It's a sorry sight to watch a man who has everything fritter his good fortune away because of his downright suicidal instinct. A precarious view of himself keeps him walking tightropes of dangers on which he must prove his physical skill and his manhood. Eventually the challenge is lost, and he falls and is ruined.

Fortunately, in magic there is sometimes a recourse when mistakes are made. Not always, mind you, but sometimes. You can lose your life in a magical accident, just as surely as you can on skis or in a car. But in cases where, because of an ill-performed spell, you've cursed yourself into being a social pariah, or turned Lady Luck into a terrifying banshee, there's hope.

My advice to you, if you've become the victim of a magical act, is to seek out a gypsy wise woman. You'll find there are gypsies almost everywhere, if you take the trouble to look for them. There's a community in New York City, and another on the West Coast. There are gypsies in the South. Ask people, and you'll find them. A wise woman has the power to cast off the evil eye.

When a person stares at you with hatred or envy, he's working the evil eye on you. When, because of a magical backfire, everyone stares hatefully at you, you're at the mercy of an enormous black power. It may be that you will want to reinforce the gypsy's magic with some more of your own. Have a witch friend do the following spell to aid in ridding you of the evil eye:

Begin by having the witch draw a magic circle about you at midnight, outdoors, in the earth. She should draw the circle with a willow wand, saying as she does:

> Spirits of the Earth, of Fire
> Of the Air, of Water
> Stay you!
> Come not here.
> Back from the circle,
> Touch it and suffer the
> Wrath of Heaven.

Then she should draw about the circle another one made with salt. And on the salt circle, at intervals, she should place garlic. This done, she should sit, facing north, outside the circles and burn evil-smelling herbs (such as assafoetida) in a chafing dish. The accompanying incantation goes:

> The Evil Eye is on thee,
> Out, Evil Eye.
> The Evil Eye comes out of thee,
> Away, Evil Eye.
> Take yourself from this man,
> Away from this man, Evil Eye.
> Come out at once,
> Or I'll poison you with stronger fumes,
> Come out at once,
> Or I'll whip you with my wand,
> Out, Evil Eye,
> Away from this man.

This spell should be repeated three times, or until there is visible evidence that the evil eye has been removed (you will suddenly feel, if it's gone, as if a great load has been removed from your mind).

Now what you must do is try to make yourself more attractive to the women you meet. Immediately make up a batch of the following perfume: mix one part musk and one part patchouli. (The odor is a little strong, so wear it sparingly.) You'll find yourself an absolute magnet to girls.

Once you do have someone interested in you again, you might wish to use some magic aphrodisiac, or a little love spell. But be careful this time.

CHAPTER V

To Preserve a Witch's Sanity

⋖§ To Catch Birds ૬⋗

Within the last year or so there has been a big movement in New York among single girls to share their apartments with single men, and vice versa. There are no studies available on why living together has suddenly become so popular at this particular moment in history. I attribute it mostly to the high cost of living and the dissipating Victorian morality about such matters.

What's also going on, though, is that everyone has suddenly become pet happy. And people say that they've acquired their animals because it's nice to have another living soul around the house. So maybe the phenomenon is really that it's no longer unthinkable to admit you're lonely. In New York, where people are practically living in each other's laps, a lack of friends is especially frustrating because all around you are people. Obviously enjoying themselves. Coping with the frustration, stoically and alone, has, up to now, been a national city pastime.

In the matter of pets, poodles are still the favorites. Parrakeets belong to the half-crazed. German shepherds are owned by those who live in dangerous sections of the city, or by fraidy-cats, or by people with valuables to guard. (One fellow I've heard about has a timber wolf with piercing yellow eyes.) Cats are, currently, the acceptable pets in the city, and girls as well as men without an image problem own them in profusion. Persian, Siamese, and Himalayans, as well as nondescript alley types, are okay.

But I think it would be lovely to wake to the song of a wild bird on a gray, gloomy Monday. It's illegal to capture them in this country, no matter how tenderly you plan to treat them. But if the urge to share their sound and spirit is irresistible, here's the way to lure them:

> Take six hairs from your head and lay them across the opening of a silver cup in which you've put a solution of rainwater and sugar. If a bird should drink it, its soul will belong to you forever.

❧ To Break a Fever ☙

You would think that in this enlightened day and age it would be a simple matter to get a doctor to visit you when you're sick. Not so. If you're lying in a bed of pain, your temperature soaring, your mouth crisping from the heat, just try to get a doctor to come to your abode. It's virtually impossible. All you'll get on the telephone is sympathy and an admonition to dress warmly when coming to the office, as the temperature outside is below zero. How, you wonder, can you dress warmly when you're out flat and couldn't possibly lift even a pinkie?

In New York, the situation isn't as serious as it is elsewhere, because of an organization called the Doctors' Emergency Service. If you're seriously incapacitated, all you have to do is call the number and sometime within three hours a physician will appear. This is not to say, however, that the woman taking your call doesn't interrogate you carefully: "What should I tell the doctor about your illness? Is it possible for you to get to a hospital? Our doctors are very busy, you know."

In the smaller cities, however, no such organizations exist. You just get out of bed, whether or not you're up to it. For unfortunate sufferers from severe fever, here is the famous formula to break it (just mutter it over and over to yourself, first saying it forward, then backwards, as you pull on your second pair of socks to brave the weather on the way to the wretched doctor):

Abracadabra
Abracadabr
Abracadab
Abracada
Abracad
Abraca
Abrac
Abra
Abr
Ab
A

As you drop syllables, so will your fever drop.

⋖§ To Stop a Toothache §⋗

It really pays to take vitamins and eat green leafy vegetables, even if you hate them, because it's worth your life to get sick. I mean if you get liver trouble or a case of the roaring hives (these can be quite unbearable), or develop an extra kink in your small colon, you might survive the hospital bills if you have insurance. If you haven't got any, forget it.

Equally insidious, and devastating to a bank account, can be encounters with the dentist. Nobody ever talks about the miserable bills that dentists hand out, but they most certainly are jawbreakers. And no insurance for extensive dental care is easily available. All of us are virtually naked, financially, when we go to the teeth men, exposed to what seem the arbitrary totals of egomaniacs drunk with power. Happy on their own laughing gas, perhaps.

So it always comes as an annoying shock when I get those superfriendly little cards: "Time for your half-yearly checkup." Visions of white-coated demons leap in my thoughts, poised above my parted lips, forceps at the ready, dollar signs glinting in their eyes. I don't think I've ever willingly honored a half-yearly checkup.

It's a doubly nasty shock, therefore, when, two years later, the dentist having given me up for lost, a tooth begins to ache. How dare that tooth throb? What horrendous bills it presages. Nevertheless, I overcome the pain and stay away from the dentist for as long as possible. It is for this period of malingering that I've found the next charm an absolute lifesaver. It makes a toothache stop. With its good offices, I have been known to put off the dentist for a full month (which is really foolish, as you know, because by then it's time for a root-canal job on the tooth). Never mind. Dentists of the world, turn over in your graves. Here's the magic charm to eliminate a tooth pain. Say loudly and clearly:

> Pain in my tooth go away
> Or the Black Mummy of the
> Great Tomb will take you.

⚜ To Protect Valuables ⚜

If you've ever owned a very valuable piece of jewelry, you know that along with the joy you have in possessing it comes the concern you get from worrying about it. You're sure that every burglar in town must know that you have this jewel, and before long one of them is going to get it from you.

Have you ever tried to find a secret place in your room to hide something? No matter where you go—to the dresser, the bookshelf, the bathroom, the kitchen—you're positive that any burglar would search there, too. You can almost feel his hot breath on your neck as you tape your treasure to the underside of the wash stand. You can almost see his beady eyes light up with glee as you push your jewel beneath the rug under your bed. There are very few places in this world to be private, let alone hide a possession.

My parents have a French friend who ran messages for the underground during World War II. Once, he told my father, he had to leave an important paper in the house where he lived with his mother while he went out of Paris for a few days. So he gave the paper to his mother and said, "Where do you think the Germans would be least likely to look for this if they came to the house? You hide it, and I will see if I can find it." She thought for a long while, then put it in the frame of a photograph on her dresser. When he came into the room, he went straight to the photograph on the dresser and removed the paper. His mother cringed, terrified. So he took the paper, put it in a wrapping, and went outside to the back porch. Over the door in the back was a ledge, and on that ledge he hid the package. The Germans did, in fact, visit his house while he was away, but they didn't find the paper.

If you have a jewel, and wish to keep it safe, use the following spell to protect it from thieves.

Walk eleven times around the object, and repeat at every turn:

> Safe from harm,
> Who breaks this charm
> Will fall away,
> Then disappear to dust.

৵৽ *To Amuse Friends* ৽৽

Life as a witch wouldn't be much fun at all if all you ever
did with your craft were deadly serious things like getting
the man you want in your clutches, or making life unpleasant for your enemies. These are works of the greatest moment, of course, and the only really good reasons for being a
witch in the first place. But sometimes it's nice just to be
amusing, to do things that make you and your friends laugh
a little.

Take a lovely, starry summer night, for example. There
you are with a bunch of people on some distant, warm and
moonswept beach, having a little fire with roasted hot dogs.
You've been cavorting about, swimming and having water
fights and burying people in the clammy sand, drinking beer
and listening to someone strum a guitar. As the party dies
down a bit, you decide it's time to bring on your act. You've
brought with you some dried lucuma, a fruit that grows in
Chile (have a friend who is skiing at Portillo bring you
some). When you cast some lucuma in the fire, everyone
will be startled to find the sky convolving and all the stars
whirling and dancing and leaping about as if they were fire-
flies flitting over black water. The heavens will seem to be a
mass of whirling pinwheels, and if that spectacle doesn't
amuse your companions, then nothing ever will, and you'd
better find some new ones.

And if you should ever be with your friends out in the
country having a picnic in some splendid summer meadow,
with clover and flowers to perfume the air as you while away
the hours beneath a spreading shade tree, then try this funny
trick for them:

Prepare a charm of clover flowers, honeycomb, and
blood from the sole of your left foot. Make with these a

little cake (you may use ordinary flour), and put it in a box. Sometime during the course of the afternoon, take out your cake and set it on the ground in a patch of clover. After a while, everyone will suddenly become aware that a giant clover plant has sprung out of nowhere in the midst of the party and is looming ominously.

Part II

HATE MAGIC

CHAPTER VI

Practicing Black Magic

In some ways, the black magical operations that derive from voodoo are the easiest for us, as Americans, to perform effectively. I would guess that very few people in this country—believers in magic or not—would bet their lives that voodoo has no power. (Haiti, after all, lies but a short distance from our shores, and what goes on there is common knowledge.) A great many Americans will scoff at the magic that comes from the ancient Egyptian, Assyrian, or Sumerian tradition, but when it comes to voodoo, they're not so sure. Too many tales have been told, and continue to be told, about the disbelieving white man who falls into disfavor with a practitioner of the voodoo craft and either dies or lives to regret it. In our American heart of hearts, none of us are absolutely certain that we could withstand the curse of the hungan.

Interestingly enough, the techniques used in voodoo ceremonies and those used in traditional sorcery bear a remarkable resemblance. In both cases, incantations are used, and sacrifices are employed. The voodoo priestess will often prepare herself for her magical feat by tearing a chicken to bits with her teeth, masticating the entrails. The violent death of the animal sets in motion the proper vibrations necessary to awaken the evil spirit that she wants to come down to possess her or her assistants. In traditional sorcery, when sacrifice is used, it's done, more or less, for the same purpose.

And then there's the matter of the voodoo doll, that colorful bit of wax, clay, or cloth that is made in the image of an enemy and stuck full of pins. In Celebes, in Indonesia, the voodoo doll is man size. In Haiti, it is small, as are the dolls of Europe and America. The American doll comes to us, historically, by way of Egypt, ancient Greece and Rome, and Europe, where they were much used in the Middle Ages.

Sorcery, in the old days, had for practicing magicians an almost religious significance. The intent of the sorcerer was to be one with a conjured spirit, to become as powerful as a god. When using incantations, the magician didn't conjure just vague, malevolent influences. He dealt with actual devils with such names as Baale and Asteroth. Today, it's difficult for us to think in terms of these hell creatures. In order to make sorcery work for us, we need to strip away what looks like mumbo-jumbo, and go for the commonsense aspects of the art.

For instance, an early magician, in a black ceremony, would identify with the force he was arousing. To kill someone, a magician would call down, and become, a deadly devil and with his expanded mind power actually commit murder. Now to us this is hideously repulsive nonsense. Since we know the force of magic lies in powerful projections of the mind, and in the state of satori, we've no reason, today, to want to become devils from an antique age and have them do our dirty work.

On the other hand, the ancient concept of attaching your mind power to the victim makes sound psychological sense. If you've got a bit of clothing or hair from your enemy, it's easier to sensitize yourself to him—you've an actual bit of your enemy in the room to relate to. His image comes effortlessly to your thoughts, and visualizing him clearly is, of course, of primary importance when you're bewitching.

Ancient magicians, using images of their victims, or various personal items from them, would torture these mercilessly. They would plunge their instincts to infernal depths until their hatred could be pitched against the enemy with the force of the devil. Toads were obscenely crucified upside down; henbane and other evil substances which, when burned, give off maliferous odors, were used. Often the image of the victim was drowned in poison or water. Such acts have some relevance for us (though I don't condone the toad scene), as their object is to produce a psychological state conducive to projecting, successfully, huge hatred.

In an attempt to lure down the proper devil, the ancient magician would surround himself with symbols of that devil. For example, in a ceremony of hatred or lust, the sorcerer would drape his altar in red, wear red robes, burn red candles, and so on. Again, for us, such trappings make some sense; psychologically they help set the mood for black witchcraft.

Finally, traditional sorcerers never simply spoke their incantations, but mustering every emotion, worked themselves up into that special, almost self-hypnotic, trance state, where self is forgotten and pure, strong, projected mind power takes over. Obviously, the technique is important.

I've gone over these points because while they're not so important in love spells (the emotion you feel and project then is less easily interrupted by doubts about what you're doing), they're vital in black magic, where your feelings may phonily string you along, pretending they're real hatred ones and causing you no end of trouble because they're not.

The idea of working some hateful black magic is appealing. Instead of being hurt and crying with frustration over someone's injustice, you think, "Oh, goody, no need for that—*I'll* get even." I've said, however, that mistakes in black ceremonies can kill. Whether or not devils actually, in a moment of weakness, get into you and do the damage (maybe it's really psychological repercussion, boomeranging evil intent?), *something* surfaces in a black ceremony that is ineffably malevolent. Treat the devil with respect.

The early sorcerers never called on a devil to do them a favor unless they were prepared to offer a favor in return. For followers of the traditional witchcraft religion, the price was a pact to spread the devil's word. What payment are you prepared to make?

❧ To Torment, but Not Permanently Injure ☙

There is probably someone you know who just constantly gets in your hair, and whose presence, unfortunately, can't be avoided. If you have a job, perhaps it's the girl with a position slightly more important than yours, who can't seem to speak a sentence without sounding officious. All she has to do is walk down the hall, and you know by the sound of her footsteps that she's coming your way.

There she is, being her usually ghastly self, and, of course, you defer and maintain your cool and your cheerful expression. Wouldn't it be marvelous, just once, to *do* something to make her life unpleasant (no matter that she's probably miserable, anyway, as most officious people are usually compensating for some lack). No, that's her business. Your business is that her approach is unbearable. Why should you suffer because her husband, maybe, yelled at her this morning?

Or perhaps it's this boy you've been dating. He seemed nice enough at first, but he's turned out to be insufferable. You've already told him three times this week that your social calendar is filled for the next five years, and he's had the nerve to call you again. Persistent devil. Makes you want to scream.

Then there's always the girl who stops at nothing to get your boyfriend. She tries to make him lose interest in you by spreading rumors (or even calling him up to tell him) that you're really engaged to someone else. Oh, she's a nice one. Ripe for a little black luck, wouldn't you say?

Whoever this fly on the face of your happiness might be, here's the perfect remedy:

> Rub your warts with a dead fly (come on, you must have a wart someplace). Concentrating on your enemy, stick a needle through the fly. Now hide the impaled creature someplace close to your enemy and, sure enough, she (or he) will have nice, fat juicy warts *alll* over the body in a day or two.

Imagine a beautiful summer afternoon in the Hamptons or another wealthy resort area. You're visiting someone's sumptuous house and are luxuriating on a chaise longue by the pool, your bikini covering what it's supposed to, and a cool, refreshing drink in your hand. You're talking to this extraordinarily handsome, obviously rich, and really fascinating man and purring like a cat to yourself about how clever you are to be here passing the time with him.

Now imagine a tall, strikingly beautiful girl, tanned to the teeth, feline of movement. There's a great flurry going on over her; she's just making the most spectacular pool-side entrance you've ever seen. Men are leaping off their longues to greet her; women are calling "Hellu, darling." Everyone's eyes are on her, and more than one pair of male eyes glint greedily when she slips off her beach djellaba in one graceful movement.

So that's okay, you say to yourself. So she's the competition. And then the very worst, miserable, movie/dream-like sequence takes place. She suddenly notices your rich, handsome, fascinating man and, arms open, rapidly approaches him saying, "Darling, sweetheart, we haven't seen each other in a year, we have so much to talk about. You must come sit with me and tell me all."

Oh, faint. That's the luck. Now what to do? Do you let this obnoxious woman just get away with it, let her walk off with your exciting man, the one you've figured would make an appropriate husband should it ever come to that? Or are you going to stop her?

It's very simple, really. Just remember to plan ahead and carry a little bottle of apple juice mixed with sugar with you when you're invited to such possibly lucrative parties. Just casually stroll by your enemy and sprinkle a few drops of the juice on her clogs or beach robe. This will attract mosquitoes—all sorts of them—and pretty soon she'll have to leave.

Love situations that are clichés may be dull and uninteresting as fodder for the plots of plays and movies, but in real life they are hardly boring. Psychiatrists will tell you that if you get through the first year of married life, you'll probably make it through five years. If you get to ten, you'll probably stay married for fifteen. And at fifteen, you will, in all likelihood stay together for twenty-five. These are the probabilities, the cliché realities, but for couples living together through this obstacle course of statistics, the fifth- or tenth- or fifteenth-year breakup is no cliché, but a heartbreak unique in their lives.

If you're a wife with a husband who has lately begun to come home late from the office—business is heavy now, he says—then you're probably tortured, like a million other wives, with the worry that he has another woman. Who can she be? Is she young and beautiful? Is he spending the money for your new spring wardrobe on dinners with her? How dare he be so common, behaving like every other rotten husband you've ever heard about?

If you feel like keeping him, then the thing to do is to make it impossible for him to go philandering. Cast the following spell on your "hard-working" man, and he'll have such a case of insomnia that he'll just be able to drag himself from the office to your bed, where he'll lie awake for yet another night. Keep this up for a few weeks and your troubles will be over.

> Put together a charm consisting of the body of a fly (the house variety is fine), the body of a spider and a cat's-eye stone (if it's set in a ring or necklace, it's all right). Now put these ingredients in a black box, and when he's not looking, slip the box under your husband's pillow. Not a wink he'll get.

Few women are lucky enough to escape the overwhelming tragedy of a broken heart. Most of us get stung at least once, but there are some who seem to make a career out of being constantly crushed. Without fail. It's like being accident prone.

Can you imagine the amount of hostility a consistently betrayed woman must carry about in her? It's enough to send her round the bend sometimes. At the very least, she's unhealthy. She's the woman you probably know who can't be with a man for more than ten minutes before she's finding little ways to insert pointed remarks in his witty conversation, collapsing his ego. She's fine around women, but put her near a man and she'll quietly unsheath her special set of wits and reduce him with four or five karate-chop comments. Poor man, you say. But poor woman, too. That she could have come to *this*.

Suppose that instead of walking around half-mad with hurts, this same woman could, in a private place, away from people, remove her civilized veneer, her uptight self-restraints, and work out her anger in a thoroughly uncivilized magical ceremony. Suppose she believed that the ceremony would have consequences and that she would be getting even with a specific man, or even men? Would she be quite so hostile the next time she met a possible lover, knowing that if he were cruel she could retaliate? Wouldn't some of the pressure be off? Of course most people feel only psychiatry can effect cures, but black ceremonies can lower the boiling point of enraged feelings.

If you have need of punishing a faithless lover, draw the curtains and at midnight light a candle. Take a needle and prick the candle many times, saying:

> As I prick this candle, I prick thee.
> Break your heart, unhappy be!

If you do this with every ounce of hatred in you, there's little doubt that this spell will work; your emotions will be at such a pitch you could probably cause even the most difficult, violent spells to engage. If you've never watched the consequences of a curse unfold, and if you don't forgive easily, you're in for a spectacular treat!

In the end, it really doesn't matter if you're ugly or beautiful if you feel insecure about your man. As long as you're not convinced that your charms have blinded him to all other members of the female sex, you're going to suffer tantrums of jealousy and the red-hot angers. And it doesn't matter if you have the prestige of Princess Margaret, or the money power of Barbara Hutton, or the curves of Raquel Welsh, or the super-chutzpah of Mae West. If you aren't positive that his interest fires only around you, that his glands bloom only in your presence, then you might as well give up your claims to sanity.

I'm thinking now of a fabulously beautiful Argentine girl who was brought up with mink carriage throws and nannies and limousines, and no knowledge whatever that living is something of a steeplechase—all those hurdles to leap, all that tension born of a pounding hoof, trying to win prestige, love, whatever. For years she drifted along in her luxurious cocoon, protected from struggle of any kind by her chaperones (she never even had to study much, as she's terribly bright) who, of course, went with her everywhere, especially to parties to keep an eye on any man she might talk to. She really led the life of a storybook princess—the kind who is locked in the tower. She didn't begin to become a human being until she was twenty.

That was the year her parents sent her off to Paris to live with a rich aunt and be introduced to society and the young nobleman whom they had approved as her future husband. As soon as the plane touched down at Orly, this princess's life began to change. Her blood aroused her, tingling with spring and the city, and she began to get an inkling of what being alive could mean.

The young nobleman was divine—a sophisticated, unsheltered young man, a great fun-loving fellow with lots of friends and lots of things to do. The Argentinian was swept off her feet immediately; for them both, it seemed, it was love at first sight. A great Parisian wedding was planned, and the titled guests who attended it were straight from the pages of the *Almanach de Gotha*. Before the wedding, there were balls, and weekend trips to the country estates of friends (always with a duenna in tow). After the marriage, there was a wedding trip to Madagascar, and there was the house in Paris and the chateau in Brittany to organize and rearrange.

The sweet life lasted two years. Then the Argentine discovered that her husband had a mistress. What's worse, she found out that he had *always* had this mistress, and had been seeing her since the day they returned from their honeymoon. Sheltered from the ways of men as she had been, the young wife hadn't a thought on the subject of mistresses except the she-or-me kind. She had been insulted, wronged. That was it. Divorce.

When the papers were finalized, she left Paris and came to New York. That's where I met her. She became a photographer's model and has done very well in her new career. She has also met a man, a successful young photographer, and is living with him. But this man is just as merciless as her husband was, as he's always got some other girl going on the side. Since his outside interests are well known to the Argentinian, she spends most of her time in a masochistic haze, a whirlwind of doubts and insecurities. She's a mess, unable to cope. Supremely jealous.

I think I've been able to help her a little bit, though. She's getting the hang of spell-casting now, and since she's had one or two positive successes, she's beginning to see light at the end of her very dark hall. Here's one of the spells I've taught her to use to torment any woman who comes within reach of her man:

> Steal an item of your rival's clothing (panty hose would be perfect) and wrap in it some henbane. Now dip it in ashes and bury it in the earth. With proper concentration and projection, the enemy will have no rest by night or day (especially devastating to models who rely on their rested looks).

My friend Lucy is no slouch. She's an extremely pretty girl with long, flowing dark hair, a cameo profile, and a fine set of legs. And because her father is in the brokerage business, she's able to dress fashionably and always has something new to wear. She's also smart. And she also has a good job.

But Lucy, like so many girls, unfortunately, is extremely attractive to what she calls "the reptile people." She means those short, skinny men with glasses, small round eyes, hair short and parted on the side, whose suits are baggy around the knees. Their lips are chapped, and when they peck you goodnight (that's all you ever allow) it's like kissing a snake with dry skin. (Hence, reptile people.)

Ratso, Lucy's most recent snake man, was, like all the others, upwardly motivated. That's why he fell in love with her in the first place. He hopes ultimately to snag a girl who's gorgeous, rich, brilliant, etc., so that everyone will think he "certainly must have *something*."

Because she's such a sweet girl with a kind, gentle streak in her, Lucy found *something* endearing in Ratso that made her go out with him. And it wasn't just because he took her to the theater, the best movies, the most expensive restaurants (which reptile people always do to make up for their reptilianness). Perhaps it was because he told her about how he threw up on his first date because he was so traumatized. Perhaps it was because, even now, he's vulnerable. Anyway, the dating went on.

The trouble began when Ratso asked Lucy to go on a Circle Line cruise around Manhattan one Sunday, and Lucy for some reason didn't feel like it. She hates the cold, so perhaps it was a chilly Sunday, and Ratso wasn't worth getting the goosebumps over. Anyway, he became suddenly persistent (a quality that most reptile people display immediately, but Ratso had, to his credit, kept in check till that moment).

Well, if she didn't want to go on the Circle Line, would she go for a walk in Central Park? He had a lovely kite, he said, and the breeze was just right for kites. Lucy, probably still thinking of goosepimples, said she had just washed her hair, really, and didn't want to go anywhere.

Ratso continued. Well, couldn't he take her to Maxwell's

Plum for some brunch and champagne? Lucy gave in. "Champagne? Well, if you come for me in two hours, my hair will be dry." The beginning of a bad thing.

They were on their third glass of spirits when Ratso produced the ring. Mind you, their dating had been confined to once a week for two months. But out came this diamond. Wee. Microscopic. Vulnerable. Just like Ratso. Lucy just stared.

"Three glasses of champagne," she remarked later. "Remind me never to drink just three glasses of champagne again. Two, fine. Four, okay. Three, never." The smile, it seems, had begun at the corners of her mouth, worked itself into the crinkles around her eyes, and then burst over her teeth in a great, whomping, uncontrollable laugh.

Ratso, of course, visibly shrank in his too-large, creased wash-and-wear suit. His face drew in on itself, and his hands clasped and unclasped. Lucy finally got hold of herself and wiped the tears off her cheeks with her napkin. Naturally she apologized, and tried to explain. Naturally, Ratso didn't understand.

That night, the siege began. The phone rang in Lucy's apartment at midnight, one o'clock, three o'clock, four o'clock, four-thirty, five o'clock, and seven. No one was ever on the other end. Just breathing. A week went by. The same schedule every night. She couldn't leave the phone off the hook, because there was grave sickness in her family and she was afraid she'd miss an important call. She also couldn't believe that Ratso would keep up the barrage.

Saturday night came. I gave Lucy the following spell to perform to rid herself of the Ratso plague. It's to torture an enemy severely.

Take a candle (black is preferable for this spell) and wrap around it some item belonging to your enemy (his handkerchief, necktie, suspenders, whatever he's left behind or you can steal). Now set the candle in your bathtub (no need to set your abode on fire) and light it. As the item belonging to your enemy burns (concentrate on his face, of course), he'll begin to shiver. Wherever he happens to be, he won't stop shaking until the candle burns out.

True, it's becoming less and less fashionable to get drunk on alcohol (and, conversely, more and more fashionable to get high on hash or grass), but nevertheless, alcoholic drunkenness is still the popular escape among the vast majority of the country's population.

Judging by the numbers of people who take pleasure in occasionally getting drunk, a little escape every now and then, it would appear, seems to be good for people—or, at least, not excessively harmful to them. We seem, as human beings, to *need* to disappear once in a while into that fine, filmy glaze brought on by too much beer or wine or Scotch, where we think deep thoughts or, perhaps not thinking at all, dance over the table tops. Liquor, after all, does make it possible to express joy at a bit of good fortune in a completely uninhibited fashion, and when it's necessary to cry— only it isn't good form—wine in our veins makes us cry anyway and have done with it.

When my friend Rosemary has too much to drink, she turns argumentative, and her husband, thinking her a very unpleasant woman to have about at such times, has turned her off at the faucet. A strict rule in her house: no getting high and being bitchy. But think how *you* would feel if you knew you might never be able to drink excessively again. You might even start thinking about packing brandy in a flask and calling it your medicine!

She's fixed her husband, anyway, and is back to being

argumentative whenever she pleases. I helped her lay a trap
for him, and I recommend this to any witch who has a man
around who can't stand her when she's had too much. Just
wait until the next time *he* gets spiffed at a party or with
company, then tell him he's being an obnoxious drunk and
slap the following cure on him:

Make him drink from a bottle of Chinese wine in
which a snake is preserved (check out Chinatown for
this item). The brew is an aphrodisiac to the Orientals,
but to him it will simply appear that you're trying to
freak him out with a grisly-looking snake in a bottle
(chances are that's just what will happen). If you hate
snakes, you'll have to be single-minded to effect this
cure.

✒ *To Cause a Lot of Agony* ✑

I don't know why it is, but Suzette, my dearest friend, is
forever having long, beautiful relationships with men who
then, out of the blue, turn around and marry someone else.
What's worse, she's *always* being invited to their weddings.
Even more ghastly, she's usually still in love with the creep
when the inevitable invitation comes. And, hopeless maso-
chist that she is (at least I diagnosed her as such before the
light dawned), she *goes* to the weddings.

Now you may recall that I mentioned Suzette earlier on.
She's the supremely talented girl who has such a powerful
evil eye that all she really has to do is say "I want so-and-so
to break his leg skiing" and he does. How she came by her
superb natural evil ability I'll never know. She's a Scorpio,
but she was raised in a strict Catholic family, attended a
strict Catholic high school, and went on to a super-strict
Catholic women's college. With all that religion, how was

she able to rise above her background and keep her evil *intact*? I can't imagine. Remarkable. She truly impresses me.

Now about Suzette and her weddings. The first time a heart-throb put her on his invitation list, we were both utterly horrified. (What bad manners, just for a start.) We could hardly believe it, because the boy was the sweetest (we had thought) human being imaginable, with big, dreamy, soft blue eyes. He not only used to read Suzette poetry while they lolled on the grass in Central Park in the summertime, he used to bring wine and flowers to cheer her on wintry days. What possessed him? That was the reason Suzette went to his wedding (or so she told me). She just wanted to find out that little thing.

It was, evidently, some bad luck spirit. She came home immediately after the wedding with the most horrifying tale about how, as the divinely happy couple were emerging from the cathedral, the boy accidentally stepped on his bride's train, lost his balance and, pulling her with him went somersaulting down the very long flight of stone steps—all the way to the bottom. The bride was knocked out cold, her gown was a shambles, her veil in shreds, and her body bruised and bleeding. She had dirty great scratches and gouges all over her face. Aside from being totally mortified, the groom suffered a broken arm and a severely twisted neck. He was taken away in an ambulance—as was his bride.

Because the bride had some internal hemorrhaging, the honeymoon had to be postponed indefinitely. We learned later that just one month after that fateful day, divorce papers were in the works. She evidently couldn't stand being married to such a clumsy man.

When the second wedding invitation came in the mail, announcing the marriage of Suzette's current lover to some

San Francisco dolly, we simply stood and stared at each other openmouthed. This was, surely, one of the nastiest hands that Fate had ever dealt anyone. *Two* lovers, with no warning whatsoever, marrying *other women*. Just not to be borne. Especially by Suzette. In her angry eyes I began to see a hint, only a hint, mind you, of the truth. I wasn't sure about it, however, even though she dressed with relish in new clothes to attend the wedding.

Such a splendid wedding, she told me later. One of the attractions of the handsome fellow had been his money, and indeed, lots of it, she said, was apparent in the infinite number of bottles of vintage champagne and fresh Russian caviar that were lavished on the reception guests at his private club. (His bride—she shuddered as she said it—had no class at all and obviously no money. Her gown and bridesmaids were indescribably tacky.)

It was a pity, Suzette remarked in her most offhand way, that the bride had got a toast wedge with caviar on it lodged in her throat and had fainted dead away. They had had to carry her off to the ladies' room and call a doctor. And such a shame, Suzette continued, that the groom became so flustered, while driving his bride and the doctor to the hospital, that he got into a terrible accident. It seems he had grabbed one of the limousines out front (no chauffeurs in sight, of course, as they were off having a shot at a local bar), and forgot how *big* the car was. Tried to squeeze between two buses on Fifth Avenue. They were all badly hurt. Suzette, I could tell, felt really dreadful about the doctor. She said, "I didn't mean . . ." and then seemed to remember herself.

When her third lover's wedding invitation arrived, we both sat for a long time in the living room without speaking. Then Suzette began to cry. This surprised me, because in all the years I've known her, I've never seen a single tear dribble from her eye. Now, however, she bawled.

I comforted her as best I could—mostly by leaving her alone to feel justifiably sorry for herself—and brought her a cup of tea. Fearing for the future, I questioned her about the other weddings, when the moment was right. And, of course, she was vulnerable and admitted it. She had caused the accidents.

I didn't argue with her. I used gentle persuasion. "Suzette," I said, "don't you think that your revenges are a mite *strong*? I mean, all you really need to do is make their marriages unhappy, end in divorce, don't you? It really isn't necessary to cause these people, along with innocent bystanders, gross physical harm. Why don't you let me provide you with a little direction in your black revenges, and make them a wee bit less physical?"

In the end she took my offer. I think she was still feeling guilty about the doctor, who incidentally, suffered a broken back in the limousine accident. Here's the Witches' Ladder spell I gave her to take to her third lover's wedding, to perform during the nuptial vows. (Naturally, he divorced the girl within three months of marrying her.)

Take with you a piece of white yarn. Throughout the wedding ceremony, concentrate on the groom's face (visualize him while his back is turned) and make a series of nine knots at equal intervals on the strand. As you tie each knot, draw a cross over your heart with your left ring finger and say:

As this marriage is begun
I curse it till it comes undone.
Knots of anger, knots of hate
Make unhappiness their fate.

It won't be long before the couple's wedding day is a bitter memory.

I can't think of any other animal that is as maliciously cruel as *Homo sapiens* when he sets his mind to it (although he's usually even more vicious when he doesn't). So it's understandable that the victim of evil should be just as virulent when he seeks revenge. A vicious circle, as we say.

One of the cruelest examples of mental torture that I've ever come across took place at a party (of all places). A joyous occasion at first, it degenerated into a scene. It was the night of the eclipse of the sun, and we all later agreed that, somehow we had been victims of that eclipse—a kind of madness had issued from it. Our primeval animalism, our uncivilized selves, surfaced that night, and for two people, especially, it was a time of nightmare.

A seemingly happily married couple came to that party, and while they had no children, they'd lived in relative peace for ten years. They always told people they were content with each other, and we certainly believed them. They traveled together everywhere, and had promising careers and a lovely apartment. They always went to the theater and movies and belonged to the museums, and just generally enjoyed each other's company.

During the first part of the evening they went about and met people, chatting as you do at parties, laughing a lot, with their arms around each other. But at some point they began to drift apart and joined separate groups. The wife danced with a few people, and the husband cornered a very pretty girl, got her some champagne, and began to settle in for a talk.

It was perhaps midnight when the wife went to see about a refill for her drink in the kitchen. There, in a dark corner, was her husband . . . with the girl. I don't think I've ever seen anyone so shocked.

Immobilized by the sheer enormity of what was going on,

the wife wandered about the party, looking at people, round eyes dazed. She finally went to the bedroom and got her coat. I watched her leave. Not long after, the husband left with the girl.

A few weeks later I learned that the night of that party was the end of one marriage and the beginning of another. The husband didn't return home until the following Tuesday night, and then, I understand, it was only to collect his clothes. He moved out. Entirely. Left his wife, his life, his whole ten years of marriage behind him. Just like that.

The wife, of course, was left without one vestige of anything. I even heard that she had been hospitalized for a while. I saw her once on a street corner, and she certainly had all the earmarks of a basket case—she narrowly escaped being run down by a bus as I watched.

No one ever really knows what goes on in other people's marriages. The happiest ones, to the outsider, usually turn out to be the very worst. Anyway, the wife bumbled along for a few months, and then I heard that her husband had asked her for a divorce. All that time he had been living with the new woman; he never seemed to care a bit what happened to his wife. Any way you slice it, that's cruelty.

When the divorce was granted, the husband married his new girlfriend within a few days. The ex-wife was left with bills, an expensive apartment that she was unable to afford, and not a single tangible amenity to show for ten years of her life. That's cruelty.

So I gave her the following spell to perform:

If the faithless lover marries another, the woman should write on an egg shell, in blood, the following symbol. Then she should bury the shell in earth where the enemy often walks. This will make the marriage unhappy, and the husband will continually pine for his lost love.

If you have an enemy who is married, one of the very
nastiest spells you can cast is one that will make husband
and wife learn to loathe each other. Almost every marriage is
vulnerable, and with you picking away at your enemy's, it's
sure to dissolve in a whirlwind of oaths.

As always, you want to be sure that your punishment fits
the crime. If you meet a man and you're attracted to him,
and then you discover he's married, it would be a definite no-
no in my book if you cast a spell to break up his marriage
just to have a little fling with him. Although if you're really
evil, and amoral about such things as snitching husbands, I
guess you want what you want when you want it, and you'll
cast your spell anyway.

To give you some idea of the scope of misery that can
sometimes accompany the ruination of an enemy's connubial
bliss, witness this sad story. A not too attractive (and not too
stable, either) witch fell in love, a few years ago, with a man
who is one of those sleek, worldly creatures with shiny, rich
man's hair who regularly commutes to Hong Kong and
Manila on business, then stops in Tahiti for a rest. The witch
soon found out that this man was married, and she told a
mutual friend she once glimpsed his wife meeting him in a
car in front of his office. The wife had long, golden hair, a
sable coat, and a radiantly beautiful face, evidently. They
looked wonderfully happy together.

This witch was one of those unhappy girls who sometimes

meet appealing men, then, without a prayer of ever having them, fall in love anyway. Girls like this usually pose no threat to the object of their affections, but if the girl is a witch . . .

Well, this one soon let her loving from afar degenerate into a hounding act. She was possessed—unable to think, with his face always in her mind. She began to call him and ask to see him. She would lie in wait on street corners, then accost him and beg him to stay with her. And once she even sold her possessions, every earthly item she owned, and bought an air ticket to Hong Kong on a flight she knew that he was taking. She shadowed him to his hotel, then threw herself at his feet in his room and begged for his attentions.

The poor man. He was at his wits' end. He took the girl down to the bar, got her a drink, and asked her what in the world she was doing. She evidently poured her heart out to him in such a way that he was touched by her plight. She finally got her wish and they stayed together.

After two glorious nights (for her; I can hardly speak for him), the man suddenly disappeared. The witch came back from a shopping expedition and he was gone—bag and baggage. Her fury knew no bounds. She ripped drapes with her bare hands and slashed the carpet and bed to pieces with a knife. When the hotel manager appeared, roused by the uproar, she turned on him and he barely escaped being stabbed in the face. The police came and put her in a straitjacket and hauled her off to the hospital.

Weeks later, the girl was well enough to leave, and she took a job as a secretary to pay her hospital bill. But she seethed and burned inside, still quite insane. She began to make excursions to Hong Kong's darker streets, to its shadier districts, and soon had a collection of potions and implements that could destroy a navy. Her debt at the hospital paid, the girl boarded a plane and returned home.

Back in the city, she sought out our mutual witch friend and begged for a couch to sleep on till she could afford an apartment again. My good-hearted friend couldn't refuse, so the girl moved in, potions and pills and all.

At first the girl was reticent with her hostess about the contents of the boxes and bottles in her suitcase, but eventually her insanity loosened her tongue, and pridefully she set out her collection. My friend was impressed. She had never seen so many death-dealing magical objects in one place at one time. Then she became suspicious. It wasn't hard to get the girl going, and my friend soon learned how the objects were to be used. All night long the girl raged, screaming her hatred at that two-timing man, and all night long my friend, horrified, tried to persuade her to change her mind about the death sentence.

At last, with the dawn, my friend was able to quiet the girl. By the next afternoon, she was ready to accept a plan to break up the man's marriage instead of killing him. My friend arranged the ceremony, and that night it was accomplished. We learned that two weeks after the spell was cast the man and his wife separated. The girl is back in a sanitarium, and it may be years before she's able to come out again.

The spell the witches cast that night to destroy the man's marriage goes as follows:

Go to a cemetery at midnight and pick flowers from three separate graves. Now take some of your hair and tie the flowers together in a bouquet. Then, laying the flowers on a grave on which the moon is clearly shining, speak the following prayer:

Oh beautiful Venus, look down on me
And hear my prayer.
Take from [speak his name]

His wife [speak her name]
So that they depart from each other
In anger, in hatred,
As the sun is separated from the earth
And burns it with fiery deserts,
As the seas are separated from the earth
And drown it with billowing floods,
As the night and day never meet,
Let them meet not again.
Oh, Venus, who scorns unfaithful lovers,
Torture the weapons of my misery
[Say his name and his wife's name]
So that my revenge is yours.

Now take the flowers from the grave and go, straight away, to your victim's house and hang them above his door.

⊰§ *To Maim and Kill* ৡ⊱

Let me warn you right away that not everyone can practice black death magic. Unless there is a seriously dark side to your soul, you might just as well forget about doing people in. The only person you'll do in will be yourself.

It's ever so much easier to work positive spells, because you're dealing with emotions that you've been taught are proper and acceptable to feel. Negative feeling, hatred, just isn't in the Christian tradition; furthermore, our culture makes it painful to *dislike*, let alone hate, someone. For instance, people drop their eyes when you say, "Oh John, I can't *stand* him." You've violated a taboo. (Think how kindly people speak of that wonderful girl who never says bad things about anyone.) Breaking taboos leads to guilt, which most of us own in quantity. Do you honestly think you can overcome your Christian heritage to the extent that you can, without guilt, purely hate someone? You have to be able to do this if you want to work death spells.

The reason for needing to overcome guilt generated by feeling enormous hatred for someone, of course, is that the guilt will get in the way of casting your black curse. With even a passing guilty feeling, you will interrupt yourself in the midst of raving an incantation and think, "Oh, my God, this can't be *me* doing this . . . not nice, sweet me who was brought up with love and the good things in life . . . me, behaving like this, trying to *murder* someone . . . of all things . . . you get life or the electric chair for *murder* . . . what kind of a creep am I?"

The spell is broken. You've put yourself in danger. Evil forces, conjured in the ceremony, are constantly looking for chinks in the armor of the sorcerer, and once inside, will kill if they can. At the very least, they'll cause madness. That's why you must be absolutely certain of your blackest self— its limitations—if you're going to do this kind of thing.

It's only a matter of time before you come across someone on whom you would definitely like to cast a spell to cause some harm. Perhaps the person deserves to be afflicted with a mighty itch. Perhaps he is worthy of warts. And maybe your enemy has been so unmitigatedly miserable that he deserved to be punished by a series of broken hearts. But how often, in a lifetime, do you cross swords with a man or woman who deserves to die?

Oh, it's not unusual to become so furious that, in your heart of hearts, you do wish death to an individual. But when you own the power to cause death, a great deal of considered thought is required before you make your final decision. First, you need to cool off, let yourself be distracted from your fury and death wish. After a time, if the anger subsides, you know that your enemy didn't really deserve such a black end.

In fact, the occasions when you decide that a person deserves to die are so rare that it's hard to conceive of such cases. Certainly, an inconstant lover is usually not the proper victim of a death spell—an evil one, yes; a death one, no. And someone who is irritating and constantly causing problems for you is ripe for black magic, but for death?

The circumstances where the ultimate weapon is properly used appear to be those larger-than-life ones, when you're so backed up against the wall by your enemy that you're the victim of tremendous injury. You're powerless, unwomaned, unable to make a move.

For instance, you're a kidnap victim, and between you and freedom, maybe, or life and death, is one deranged individual. You might properly do him in. Or an elderly person you love is the victim of a con man who has weaseled away every cent and has left your loved one without income, to perish. This con man deserves to die. These are dramatic cases, situations of tremendous trauma where Fate must be deflected.

I personally know of two cases where the death sentence was successfully applied by witches, and one where it's being contemplated. The first witchcraft murder occurred in California, and the adept is a friend of a woman I know in New York. This California witch and her husband were invited to a party in Los Angeles, and while they personally aren't into the drug thing, they knew that the party-givers were. When they arrived, everyone was tripping, and the host naturally offered them something. When they both said no, the host said that was okay, then suggested some wine. The woman said she wouldn't have any just then, but her husband said sure, he'd like some.

After drinking the wine, the husband began to feel peculiar. He's never taken drugs, so he didn't recognize the symptoms. Immediately, his wife suggested they leave if he really wasn't feeling well. On the street outside, he freaked out. The devil, in full regalia—red suit, horns, pitchfork—materialized and chased him up boulevard, down alleyway, over rooftop, then around and around and around some distant block. When his wife finally found him, he was cowering behind a garbage can, counting his fingers softly to himself. She took him to the hospital. Two years later he is still in a sanitarium, by turns murmuring to himself and shrieking in agony. The host at the party had put STP in the wine.

There was a time when the woman was sure her husband would recover. But after a year, the doctors told her he would probably be a vegetable for the rest of his life. It was then that she decided to murder the host of that party, and with black magic she did. He died in an automobile accident.

Only recently I heard of a Scarsdale mother, a witch, whose thirteen-year-old son was introduced to heroin by a fifteen-year-old girl, a neighbor. I understand that this woman is in such a state that she's been asking around the witch community for the most potent death spell anyone knows. I have several friends who have been approached by her, but not one of them is willing to give her what she wants. If she intends to murder this girl, she is going to have to shoulder all the responsibility herself.

The other case I know of where a death spell was successfully used involved a young witch, seventeen, I think, who lived in Tennessee, and who was married to a forty-year-old man. This girl was totally screwed up to begin with, and brought the whole ugly episode down on her own head. Nevertheless, she couldn't live with her destiny and changed it with a witchcraft murder.

The girl, after a year or two of marriage, concluded that she was miserably unhappy. Instead of doing the sensible thing and getting a divorce, she chose to take on a lover. He was young, too, and lived nearby, and since her husband commuted to a city to work every day, she had plenty of time for leisurely dalliance. Unfortunately, her husband returned around lunchtime one day and found the pair disporting themselves about the bedroom. In a blue rage, the husband picked up some fireplace tongs and beat the boy to death. He then threatened his wife with a similar end if she so much as obliquely referred to what he had done to anybody ever, even himself. In this untenable situation, the young witch chose to kill her husband with a black spell; he died within the month, from internal injuries sustained when he fell from a ladder.

As you can see, there are times when death magic can, and perhaps should, be used. Of course, in the last case, the girl should have gone to the authorities. However . . . if you ever have need of such witchcraft, here's the deadly Witch's Ladder:

> Take some string; tie thirteen knots on it. As you tie each knot, project fierce hatred at your enemy. Then arrange to put the string in his clothing. He will slowly, horribly die. The only way to remove the spell is to retrieve the string and untie the knots while saying:

> > Knots, undone,
> > Curse, undone,
> > Let [his name] live.

Every really serious witch discovers after a bit that what she needs most is a private place to keep the various tools of her trade. After all, practicing witchcraft is considered not only odd, but even downright unnatural. In fact, it can still prove extremely dangerous. In 1969, in West Virginia, ten people brought to trial a man who allegedly had been using his occult powers to seduce a number of teenagers, including a babysitter.

So you need a secluded cupboard somewhere to store the various potions you concoct. Especially when you get into collecting such ingredients as newts' eyes. (Your regular spice cabinet, incidentally, just won't do. I once heard of a girl who accidentally herbed some chicken soup with mummy's toenails.)

Of course, most of the magical additives you'll collect will be more commonplace. For black magic, you'll probably have a supply of henbane and some plain old garlic to keep off evil. For love spells perhaps you'll have rue, as well as the full panoply of spices (including narcotic roots) that are necessary for aphrodisiac recipes.

Sometimes, however, you'll have need of exotic implements. I really don't know how to break the news to you in an easy, offhand way, but would you believe coffin nails? That's what you're going to have to get, no way around it, for this next black spell from the Rumanian witches. My advice on the subject of collecting coffin nails (which I've done) is sound. Don't go alone. Whatever you do, don't foolishly go off to a graveyard in the middle of the night (which is where and when you collect coffin nails) by yourself. Presumably, you aren't going to be silly enough to try this next spell if you're a beginning witch, anyway. So, as a more practiced adept, you'll undoubtedly have witch friends. Take them with you. Also take enough shovels (my first trip out, I only took one, and guess who did all the digging?)

Now you go to the graveyard and I don't mean the metropolitan cemetery near your house. You scout out an old, moldy graveyard that nobody pays any attention to— one far out in the country somewhere. The best bets are the little family plots that usually lie out back of eighteenth-century haunted houses. Ask around; you'll hear of one.

When you and your witch friends are at the site, don't just get out of the car and start digging, if it's your first trip for coffin nails. Hang about in the car awhile, with the windows down, so you can familiarize yourself with local sounds—

frogs, cats, what have you. If you dig right in, the first owl that hoots, you'll be halfway to Arizona with a scream on your lips. Take brandy with you. Good brandy. Pamper yourself. After all, the situation is difficult enough as it is. Bring little snifters, and soon everyone will regard the night's outing as a picnic and relax.

Now out of the car, into the graveyard. Don't take just one flashlight with you (my minimum is four). Have you ever tried to dig a hole in the dark? (For security's sake, however, don't get carried away and beam the car headlights on your work. Grave robbery is a crime, after all.)

Choose a grave that's as far away from the road as possible. Set to work. Dig one, heave one. That's how it will be for a while. Then you thunk wood. Once it's exposed, dig around the sides of the coffin till it's free (did I mention that you wear jeans, and a sweatband round your forehead?), then reach around and wriggle some ropes under the edges. You don't have to break your neck pulling this coffin up over the top of the grave, so relax. Just bring it up enough to expose some nails. Now, since everyone is going to be holding this coffin in midair, you're the one who's got to take the pliers and start working on a few nails. This should not be a lengthy, time-consuming effort because if you've chosen a ripe enough grave, the wood is going to be pretty rotten in this coffin, right? Now this is important in the extreme. If you somehow get flustered between the grunts and groans of your straining friends and the nervousness you'll feel at prying out old ugly nails from such a distasteful object, and you forget to say the following words, you can simply forget the entire effort. Your nails, when you go to use them, will be less than worthless. They'll simply be rotten bits of metal that you can't even pound into a two-by-four.

Whatever you do, remember to repeat this spell during the nail-drawing:

Coffin nails,
Familiars of maggots, worms,
And unsavory creatures of the kind,
Do my bidding,
My evil works
When I command you.

Okay. Now you've got what you're after. Don't flee the scene with your heart in your throat at what you've been doing. Stay where you are and *fill in the grave*. If you don't you'll never be able to return to this cemetery again, and who wants to be bothered with scouting out new locations all the time? Add some dry leaves, branches, acorns, whatever is about, to your nice neat handiwork, and no one will ever be the wiser.

Back in your witch's workshop, preserve your nails in a little box till they're needed. When the occasion arises—for example, a wicked witch puts the double whammy on you, trying to kill you—then bring out one nail and perform the following:

Take some personal item belonging to the enemy (this could be clothing or hair from his head) and pound one of the nails through it. While doing this say:

May [speak the name of the person you wish to do in]
Suffer the terrors of the grave,
And may he never more have hope or love
While he lives on this earth.
May he depart from here
When the moon changes.

Now the enemy is done for. Should you, for some unforeseen reason, decide that you want to remove the spell, take out the nail and wash the item belonging to your enemy in salt water to which sulfur has been added.

In the days before Freud, life was quite simple. If you were a bit odd, you were either thought to be eccentric— and accepted as such—or you were drummed out of polite society and found companionship in a circle of people who were also peculair. You were simply judged on the basis of your deeds. If you murdered, you were a murderer (not criminally insane). If you were raving mad, but clever about it, you were regarded as a saviour and heralded; if you were raving mad and picked butterflies out of the air, you were locked up. Yes, life was simple then.

Now, everyone's a psychiatrist. If you're a little odd and compulsively hum to yourself, the fellow sitting next to you on the bus will decide that you're a paranoid schizophrenic and give his seat to some unsuspecting old lady. If you smile at strangers on the street in a big city, they figure you're a homosexual and cross to the other side. If you're a woman with a loud voice, you're a castrating female. No man will give you the time of day.

What tightropes we walk! In order to be acceptable we must conform (in far more deadly ways than we've yet fully perceived) to standards of behavior. A boy without long hair, without experience of drugs and freaking out, is really thought to be abnormal by his contemporaries. The old generation thinks that showing idiosyncrasies in public is an unforgivable cultural *faux pas*. You haven't conformed to their acceptable mental mores. In their view, only the sick display aberrations such as living loosely and wearing wild clothes. The new generation thinks that *coolness* is the unforgivable *faux pas*. You haven't conformed to their mental mores—freedom of expression (be it bad or good, artistic or vulgar). Only the sick are uptight, unable to express their *selves*. Needless to say, one generation is as locked into its concepts of normal behavior as the other. When will we ever really be free? When will we ever be able to say "Who cares?" and mean it?

For those dark souls who are free of the influences of both generations, and who are therefore sick, sick, sick, here's a wicked way to kill an enemy:

> Impale a spider with a pin. Drown it in the blood of a black hen. Your enemy's death, in similar agony, will follow.

What happens when you die? . . . the *other* side, what? The other side, however, is many places to many people. And this is a most unfortunate state of affairs, because if we all agreed, we might have truth. But there is no truth—how sad.

There is a marvelous system in Catholicism that includes a hierarchy of saints (somewhat like the sorcerer's devil's hierarchy of old) that allows the Virgin, as well as various saints, to intervene in behalf of an individual. There is, in Catholicism, a sense of the fitness of things, a place for every body. Most bodies, however, find their way from purgatory to hell. What a place.

Then there is the other side in the Oriental religions, which to me represents the ultimate frustration: reincarnation. Just as you've got rid of your mind, with all its foibles and kinks, it comes back to roost in another form. What a place to be—your same old head.

The spiritualists believe that beyond this life there is another plane, a place where you go soon after death, and remain till you move on—toward the Almighty. Limbo, what a place.

Every religion has the ultimate goal of your soul all plotted out the minute it leaves your body. Such a diversity of places where it's supposed to go! Such confusions! No one in our Western culture is quite sure if he'll wind up in some sky-blue place of pastures and plenty, or in a red cellar of flames and ghastly torture, or in a gray-green place of nothingness.

I've known some people who have died and come back to tell about it. Their stories are essentially the same.

One man I knew drowned twice. Both times he had the same experience. First, there was the horrible truth of not being able to cope with the water. It came and surged and suffocated and enveloped him. When he realized it wasn't going to free him, that he was trapped by a force that he couldn't control, panic set in. He was alone against the water. He struggled, fought his way through the waves, surfacing, gulping breaths of air. But the air was really water, and he was taking it in and flushing his lungs full. When he knew that he was finished, that the water had bested him, that there was no hope of conquering it, he gave up.

Then his life passed before him. (How many times have we heard that phrase? Who has ever looked into just what it means to have your life pass before you?) And when his life, in Technicolor images, had run completely through his mind, he relaxed. He knew the end was near. Then something strange began to happen. He floated in colors—pastel shades, clouds of misty pinks and blues and whites. He knew, as the colors faded, he was dead. He was floating away from his body. His mind was free.

Both times he drowned. Both times he was revived with artificial respiration. Both times he lived to tell of his experience.

The other individual I knew who almost died was a girl, who also nearly drowned. She gave the same symptoms: an assurance that she could overcome the power of the water (it-couldn't-be-happening-to-her feeling). Then, realization that she couldn't overcome it. Fear of her fate. Then, total relaxation about it. That *was* her fate and no way to change it. She had a completely relaxed body, she told me, and a

relaxed mind. Her life passed before her. She said it began
several years in her past and worked up to the present—just
the highlights, the important moments in her then few short
years. She was nine when she drowned.

Then the cloud came. It began at the edges, a dark cloud,
gathering strength, surrounding her. She floated in it. She
died. She came to life again, with artificial respiration.

> As you perform this next ceremony, think of your
> enemy and the life that will pass before him: Boil a
> black ant in oil and put it in your enemy's food. He will
> die.

We know so very little about the supernatural in this
country that it's laughable. Scientists and ESP researchers
stroke their chins and nod gravely, and speak in careful
phrases and with considered opinions about their work, and
say literally nothing. They try to surround their subject with
an aura of respectability (to keep themselves untainted by
criticism), and try to explain psychic phenomena in palata-
ble scientific terms. They study case after case of ESP and
draw few conclusions. Where is the scientist who, for example, will patiently sit still and wait to measure a recog-
nized psychic's brainwaves when the psychic *really* starts
telepathizing, or seeing into the future, naturally? Where are
the scientific brains (with which our country abounds) who
will get into ESP research and make it a truly legitimate
study?

Other, less backward, cultures hold daily discourses with
spirits and devils. There is nothing unusual or outrageous or
inexplicable in what they do. Their minds are in tune with
forces that they take for granted, and these forces serve
them at will. We're uptight, rigid in our ideas (assuming
that magic-oriented cultures are ignorant ones, for ex-

ample), listening only to the voices that explain what we see, ignoring the intuitive voices that round out our knowing.

If group-think has got you, you'll never be psychic. But if you've managed, somehow, to overcome your cultural training and you let your brain work on many levels, your intuition can start you on the right path to being psychic. It's there in your head, helping you on a primitive level, to feel and know and foresee. You're seldom in danger, because your instincts keep you from it. Those around you are protected, because you feel their impending troubles and issue warnings, often so subtle that they are on an almost subconscious level. Your mind is alive, and people are aware of an aura of intellectual power. You're whole.

In Brazil, where the thrall of Christianity is only partial, it is all but impossible not to understand the power of the mind eventually; there are just too many examples of sorcery at work there every day. A friend, David St. Clair, who has just returned to this country after living there for many years, told me one story of black magic that is especially interesting.

An old gentleman, a white planter and very rich, had a young and beautiful daughter who knew my friend. She was engaged to a mulatto, and the old man eventually couldn't stand it any longer and told his daughter that she must give up her fiancé or risk disinheritance. After a great deal of backing and forthing, the girl decided that her fiancé could never keep her in the style to which she was accustomed (without her father's help), and she broke her engagement.

The fiancé was enraged. He stormed at the girl and her meddlesome father, then took himself off to a witch woman and told her to cast a spell on the old man so that he would die. Then, unable to contain his vengeful delight at what he had done, he called the old man and told him that he had gone to the witch woman and that his days were numbered.

Disparagingly, the planter scoffed at this and told the young man that no hocus-pocus witch could, in a million years, have the slightest effect on him. He was no backward mulatto, after all.

Blood and tailfeathers. The ex-fiancé called on the witch woman again and told her what the planter had said. Furious, she went around to the planter's house and told the old man that he'd see just what kind of a phony she was. He threw her out. From the doorstep, she screeched that from now until the day he died he'd see an old woman who would just sit near his house and stare at it. He'd find out who was phony.

The next morning, as the planter left for his office, he noticed an old woman sitting on the curbstone opposite his house—just staring at it. He came home that night, and there was the same old woman. Just staring at his house. Next morning, sure enough, he glanced out the window and the old woman sat there, implacably staring. Before he got into his car to head for his office, the planter accosted the hag and asked what a foul old woman was doing in this rich man's neighborhood, staring at a rich man's house. The hag slowly rolled her eyes upward to where the planter stood, stared at him a moment, then turned them slowly back to the house.

That night, the planter could stand it no longer. He couldn't eat his dinner and he called his wife to the window and told her that he was going to call the police and have that woman removed, since she had been sitting out front there for several days. The wife looked up and down the street and said that she saw no one there. Who was he talking about?

That did it. Next morning, the planter decided to run his car over the hag, who was still sitting there, staring. He roared out of the driveway and ran directly over her and hit a tree. When the police came, the planter was raving. He had killed an old woman accidentally, he cried. The police looked everywhere and found no body.

Weeks went by. The hag continued to stare at the house. The old planter grew thin and hysterical. His wife kept the window blinds pulled. Then, one morning, on rising, the planter threw up the shade in his bedroom and let out a scream. The old woman was gone . . . those were his dying words.

A hate joke? Black magic in Brazil. Macumba. Who, in our culture, can fully understand such power?

One of the most effective, and classic, methods of killing a human being with magic is to make a wax doll in the shape of the person (and with his features). And when you want him to suffer greatly in an arm or a leg or in his head, then take a pin and pierce the doll in that part. And if you want that person to die, slowly, agonizingly, then light a fire and let it melt that part of the doll away which will eventually kill him (its head, its limbs). And when the doll is entirely melted, he will be dead.

The criminal mind holds a deep fascination for me, as I guess it does (judging from the popularity of books and TV programs about crime) for a good many people. Perhaps the reason we're crime buffs, so enthralled by the subject, is that we're trying to fathom whether we, too, are capable of a large-scale criminal act—murder, specifically. Often, when we read about others who have murdered, a lot of us search ourselves to see if the reason he was driven to it could also drive us to it. We keep tabs on ourselves, evaluate our state of mind, make sure that we're sane and adjust the odds on whether we'll stay that way.

I've talked to people who have said, outright, that they're sure they're capable of committing murder. They have no special victim in mind, but are quite certain they could kill if a situation arose. And, sometimes, situations do arise.

I think I could kill, too, if some wretch attacked me on a lonely night street, knife drawn, and I couldn't escape. I know that I'd turn on him. I might get myself stabbed to death, but the assailant would find himself much the worse for his encounter with me.

One terribly sweet girl, a model, who has a very clever fiancé, was just recently attacked in a New York loft building by a man who came out of nowhere, followed her into the building's elevator, then drew a knife. Her fiancé had trained her always to carry a can of Mace in her hand when she walked alone at night. Her reaction was immediate and effective. One spritz from the can, and the assailant ran screaming, blinded, from the building. She was safe. (Mace, of course, is not legal for a private citizen to carry in New York.)

If Mace were legalized, there would be a dramatic drop in the number of purse-snatchers, molesters, and muggers that plague us. So why can't this be brought about? Just because there are a few trigger-happy types wandering around who would squirt the weapon revengefully or too hastily? What a shame for the rest of us. The muggers will forever be the odds-on winners. As to the dangers of the chemical when sprayed in the face, it strikes me that a mugger deserves some danger. It doesn't seem to bother the police, who use the stuff, that rioters or robbers come away with potentially impaired vision.

Ever since Janice Wylie and Emily Hoffert were so brutally murdered in their New York apartment a few years back, I've been truly a Nervous Nelly. I have not one easily accessible weapon in the house that could be used for self-protection. My kitchen knives are all in the kitchen. But I know how safe I'd feel if the law would allow me to keep a can of Mace within easy reach beneath my bed.

The public doesn't seem to comprehend the scope of hideous crimes that occur in cities. Nobody hears much about them—except as statistics in TV specials on the subject or when the police give their yearly accountings. But in the cities life is becoming increasingly cheap.

I realized just how cheap when one Sunday morning I overheard my building super discussing his whereabouts the night before with his wife. "The reason I came home so late was because I was in this bar with the guys, just having a drink, you know, when suddenly this man comes in, see, pulls a gun, and nails a guy sitting two seats down from me. When the cops came, he was already dead."

I searched *The New York Times* and *The Post* the next day. Not a printed word on the dead man. My super wouldn't lie, either. He's tough and unexcitable. A street person. Not impressed. Even when he was talking about the murder, his voice was registering only mild interest. And you don't fib about such things to your wife.

The murdered man was, obviously, a poor unknown, a nobody, I finally decided. Only middle-class victims get reported in the papers. That's the way it is. Life is cheap, and the poor are completely expendable.

What black, unspeakable urges seethe in the mind of a criminal? What possessed that English couple to kill, then chop to bits, Lord knows how many children in the famous British Moors murder case? What strange spell can possibly cancel out all thought and feeling in the human mind so that it can conceive of dismembering bodies?

At least the witches of old used their religious ceremonies as an excuse. Here is a classic witch's method for killing an enemy:

> Burn in a caldron chips of ironwood, and cast on them vervain and yarrow. Add the ashes of the ingredients to oil and as you put the mixture in a bottle say:
>
> Xapeth, Xith, Xandra,
> Zaped, Zapda, Zik.
>
> When you wish to kill someone, anoint him with the evil soot.

I keep harping on the theme that when you decide to put a death spell on someone, you should do so only after a great deal of consideration. In actual fact, if you do get carried away with the notion of doing someone in, and are anything less than a full-fledged adept, you're probably not going to accomplish your goal. If you don't, in fact, harm yourself with your magic, and actually do manage to apply it to your victim, chances are he's not going to drop dead at all, but merely fall sick.

There was a time (let's be honest) when I thought that a girl I unfortunately had to work with was eventually going to torture me to death with her incessant connivings. It was a hopeless situation. Among other things, she saw to it that I had no friends in the office. She told everyone the most God-awful lies about me, and I couldn't find a soul who would believe that she was a fruitcake and that I wasn't the livid bitch on wheels, depraved, deranged, that she'd painted me. Like some paranoids, she was a brilliant liar; I was completely at her mercy. I drooped around, an outcast everywhere, alone. But I didn't want to quit, because that would be giving in to her, and anyway, my job was excellent.

It was then that I first toyed with the idea of doing her serous injury with magic. With so much time on my hands (no friends to spend it with), I began looking into the sort of black spell that would be appropriate for me—not too ghastly to contemplate, not too horrible to do. I found one, at last, and prepared myself for the undertaking.

For several evenings prior to my ceremony, I sat around and contemplated the enemy, trying to get a bead on just how much I hated her, how much fury I was prepared to whip up and vent against her. This, I can tell you, is an exercise in honesty. You actually have to conjure up your hatred and consolidate it (though, of course, you don't project it at this stage), and if you're not a naturally re-vengeful human being, you have some bad moments. In the bad moments, however, you plumb your doubts and weigh them against your enmity, and pretty soon you figure out whether you're going to be able to go through with the black ceremony. A strong sense of fair play helps you to measure your grievance honestly against the remedy you propose for it.

On the night I was to do the ceremony, I spent several hours relaxing, first by doing stretching exercises to untense my muscles, and then in a contemplation period, to clear my mind of worry and the day. I sat for a while in front of the fire and stared into the flames, trying to imagine myself in-side them, blue and hot and tasting fresh logs. When I felt myself one with the flames, I brought the image of the girl into the scene and imagined devouring her with my white-hot flicking, and I smelled burned flesh as her cells col-lapsed.

Out of this imagining trance, I moved quickly to the ceremony. While doing it, I let my mind expand, as if it had the power of fire and fiery heat, the sun, a universe of suns, and I unfolded the spell and I hurled the curse with the force of a demon and cast it over her, a net of invisible fury, a winding sheet wrapped by a death's head, a tunic of evil, with no escape.

Slowly, slowly, I strangled her with my mind, slowly she fell limp, her face white, her mouth blue, her eyes popping; then she was slack, then dead. And I kept the image a moment, then let it drift away.

The next day, my enemy didn't feel well. She dragged herself to the office, but she felt so terrible that after an hour she decided to go home. Her face was white. She seemed listless. She complained of no specific pains, but rather of a feverish feeling. Perhaps it was flu, she said. I smiled to myself and didn't commiserate. Throughout the day, I was exultant. I was sure that her illness was my doing, and just as certain that I couldn't wait around to find out if she'd worsen on the strength of one black magic ceremony.

That night I repeated the process. I grew and grew and let my mind come out of my body in satori, and let it drift through the streets, free, unfettered by my flesh, until it reached her house. Through the wall of her bedroom I came and hovered over her bed. She lay there ill, pining. I cast hatred upon her, hot, fiery bolts of pure thought, a curse, a black, avenging, raging curse. I watched her worsen and wither beneath my all-seeing mind-gaze. I drifted away then, slowly, homeward, slowly, exhausted, and re-entered my body. I slept soundly that night. Next morning, I learned that the girl had been taken to the hospital. She was bedridden for a very long time. She didn't die, but for months she was a wraith. I must admit this: after a time I regretted what I had done.

This is not the spell I used on her; I've destroyed that one. But you know the process of bewitchment, and a first-class adept can cause death with this Witch's Ladder:

Take a red thread and tie ten knots in it while saying:

The first knot I draw is to cause (speak enemy's name) a pain in the shoulder.

The second knot is to make his legs weak so he stumbles and falls.

The third knot is for a mighty pain in his head, a searing pain, an ache to make him sick.

The fourth knot is to cause him agony in the stomach, great agony, he casts up his food.

The fifth knot is to make him impotent.

The sixth knot is to make him sick with a mighty fever.

The seventh knot is to make him cry without stopping—a storm of tears.

The eighth knot is to make his mind wander—he can't remember his name.

The ninth knot is to make him wither, his limbs wither, close to death.

With the tenth knot I cast, he is to die in pain for now and ever after.

The fear in which the voodoo doll is held is awesome indeed. Even seeing such an item on display in an occult shop will, to this day, send chills up my spine. There's something ineffable and final about the item; evil radiates from it as surely as heat does from the sun.

The advantage of working with the voodoo doll is, of course, that its meaning is universally understood. Where a victim might ignorantly quibble with you about the effectiveness of a gypsy spell that you've cast on him (should he learn that you've done so), he will not quibble about a voodoo doll.

There is a very well-known, and extremely well-to-do, society woman in New York who was, a few years ago, the victim of a voodoo doll enchantment. She was dressing to attend a charity benefit one evening, and as she was rummaging about in her stocking drawer, so the story goes, she pricked her finger. Startled, she carefully removed the layers of nylons and unearthed, toward the bottom of the pile, a peculiar little object—a tiny Raggedy Ann creature with a wax head. Bits of hair, the color of her own, were lodged in the scalp, and one tiny hand bore a wee diamond—a perfect replica of her own fabulous gem, her well-known trademark. Stuck through each cloth hand was a pin, and lodged in the stomach, a thorn. When she held the doll close to look at the face, she realized it mimicked her own.

Her throat seized up. No sound came. Then she dropped the doll and ran screaming through the house, collapsing in the library at her husband's feet (I've spoken with this man, and he says she was in deep shock by the time a doctor came).

For more than an hour, no one was able to get a word from the woman. She lay, in a trance, on the library couch. Then the doctor decided to risk moving her to her bedroom. When she was tucked in, her husband turned and noticed the open stocking drawer. Then he saw the peculiar object on the floor.

When he saw what it was, he called the doctor over. They examined the doll together and agreed that this was certainly the cause of the trouble. The doctor gave the woman a tranquilizing shot and advised her husband to take her to see a psychiatrist in the morning.

The next day, the woman was able to get up and move about, but she spoke little. When she did, it was to complain of her hands, which she said felt numb, and that her stomach pained her. By afternoon, her hands were paralyzed, and nothing short of another tranquilizing shot could stop her continuous convulsive retching. The psychiatrist came to the house.

With the help of hypnosis, the woman was able to gain some composure again. When she felt a little better, the psychiatrist took her to a witch woman who could undo the voodoo curse. Within five minutes of its removal, all symptoms of her illness had disappeared.

The witch woman also told her who had given her the doll, and made up a similar fetish that the society woman delivered with relish to her enemy next day. Tacked it above the front door of her victim's townhouse, I was told. Last I heard, her enemy was in a private hosptial, having a "rest."

If you can cope with all the evil vibrations and repercussions of the voodoo doll, here's one method of using it that will effectively dispatch an enemy:

> Make a model of your enemy in cloth and lay it in a running stream (if you live in New York, put it in the Hudson River). Anchor the doll with a stone. As it rots away, your enemy will gradually lose control of his limbs. When the doll is completely destroyed, your enemy will die. If you wish to stick pins into the doll as it lies in the water, slowly spoiling, your enemy will suffer an awful, painful death.

I think it's time that I round out your education on the subject of wax dolls. By now you're aware that this is one of the deadliest methods of doing away with enemies (if you're skillful, that is, at artistically sculpting faces). What you're probably not so aware of, though, is that you can use an image, with an accompanying death curse, to achieve just partial results—a desirable effect in certain circumstances.

Suppose that your current lover is living with you (or you with him) and that all was going well till you had your friend Sally over for dinner one night. Then you realized, too late, that this was a stupid thing to have done. Their attraction was immediate and visible; he practically ignored you, the wretch. But as the evening wore on, you became even more concerned because he suddenly stopped giving Sally his undivided attention and started giving it to you. This change in the wind occurred just after you emerged from the kitchen, where you had been doing the dishes. He had been left to entertain Sally while you were busy, and now, it was obvious, he had been doing the job too well. Sure enough, the next night around eight he said he was going out to see his friend Joe for a while. Funny, you thought, a Joe that looks like Sally.

Here's where some black doll magic can be handy. You don't want to kill your lover, you just want to incapacitate him a little (if you're not so horrendously angry that you really *do* want to kill him, that is). All you have to do is, midway in the deathly illness that will result from using the doll, withdraw the image from its hiding place and remove the curse. Meanwhile, your man's been sick, agonizing on a bed of pain, and been thoroughly punished for his misdemeanor.

Images can, actually, be made of clay, cotton, wool, wood, or wax. They can be punctured with thorns, pins, and needles. They can be placed in an oven and roasted for hours, so as the material slowly burns, the body becomes fevered and dies. They can be put in running water and as the water rots them, so will the victim perish. If a doll is pierced through the heart, the victim will die in a fortnight.

Okay. So you've been engaged to this man for some time now and, beginning last week, he stopped calling you every evening at six and stopping by every evening at seven. Something is definitely strange. You call *him* at eight, and the phone just rings and rings. Nobody home.

Your heart glazes over in anger and fear. Just where *is* that man, and what is he up to? First of all, you must try a fidelity test, and if the spell proves he's false, you're on.

Gather the actual proof of his wrongdoing. *Never* haphazardly set about to practice black witchcraft. Supposing the poor man, in order to help pay for your engagement diamond, has taken a second job selling kisses at a church bazaar and is too embarrassed to tell you about it. Just how would you feel if, after the fact of your black ceremony, you discovered his more or less innocent transgression? Not only would *you* feel bad, but *he* would be destroyed, utterly ruined, by your carelessness.

Check with your friends. Have they seen him lately? No proof from them? Walk the streets, checking out your various haunts; if he's out with another woman, he's bound to turn up somewhere with her.

Let's assume that you find them necking in the corner of that special bar that he *swore* he'd never take anyone to again if you two should break up. The red you see quickly turns to purple. Total anger, total hate. Totally, you are the woman scorned.

Now, just hang on a bit. Decide what you want to do. You can be mature about this, go home, chew your nails, have a sleepless night, and call him the next morning and demand an explanation. Never accuse at first; begin with "Where were you last night?" See if he hangs himself. Then chop him off at the feet by working a spell to bring him bad luck for the next ten years. In many ways, this approach is the best, but if you're dramatic, it is not entirely soul-satisfying.

If you're a woman with a Mediterranean temperament, perhaps you had better be true to your passion and do him in on the spot. Go right through the door of the bar and present yourself to the offending couple. Just sort of materialize before their table if you can—unbelievable drama when he looks up and sees you standing there. Now hiss at him (don't dream of screeching, the force of your words will be dissipated by your man's looking around to see if everyone else in the place is listening). Spit your words at him as an asp might, saying that you're going home to work a death spell on him. Glare evilly and melt away.

Whichever method suits you, when you do get down to it, here's the perfect black spell to cast:

Light a black candle, look into its flame, and pro- nounce the following incantation:

Black spirits of the night who
Riseth from the shadows of hell
And tormentest sinners,
Swirl about me now
And hear my command!
Go to the chambers of [here, name the beastly creep]
And cause him to burn
With the fires of everlasting damnation
For his sin against me.
Dark familiars, take his body
And knot it with pain,
With cramps that seize his throat
And stifle his breath,
And do not return till you have
Done as I've commanded,
Or I will bring the wrath of Heaven's angels on you.

If you do this spell as outlined, don't be surprised if he dies in the night.

✑ *A Full-Dress Black Ceremony* ❧

There are magicians in this world who can simply con- struct a wax image of an enemy, and with supreme concen- tration and projection, stab it with pins and cause immediate and deadly harm. There are also magicians who rely heavily on psychology when they cast a spell with a doll—they make sure that the victim hears, through the grapevine, that a pin-stuck image has been made of him. But that's cheating.

No fair. You really don't have to be a magician at all to destroy an enemy with his own fear. Furthermore, the technique is dangerous. With some inquiring around, the psychologically attacked victim can discover who's put the spell on him.

It's a much safer bet to cause havoc in total privacy and secret. Then, only the most sensitive of psychics can give the victim a clue to his tormentor's name—if, that is, he has guessed that a spell has been worked on him. And the chances of the victim's running across a truly good psychic in this country are fairly slim. The market for full-time practicing adepts with superior powers isn't really big; they can't make much of a living here. South America, the Orient, and Africa are another story, however; in those parts of the world, the truly talented psychics reside.

If you're discreet, it's not likely that you will be found out. It is, therefore, worthwhile when causing harm to an individual with a wax doll, to do so in a ceremony of extreme efficacy, relying completely on your own powers to do the dirty work.

Early European sorcerers went to a great deal of trouble to perform their secret works. The tools of their trade were all hand-made from virgin materials, because just any old implement might have been used for some purpose at complete odds with how they intended to employ it. It would never have done, for instance, to use in a magical ceremony a knife that had been peeling potatoes for years. Potato vibrations don't mix well with magical ones. A walking stick used as a wand wouldn't make it, either.

The magicians also did a great deal of sprinkling with holy water and perfuming with incense. Every time they made or used something, out came the aspergillums and censers. Their nervousness and compulsiveness in this matter are quite understandable when you realize just what little devils magicians thought conjured black spirits could be.

If there was one tiny particle of dirt or unconsecrated territory on the operator, in his magic circle, or even in the room where he worked, *voilà*, the nasty spirit pounced on it and began to take over just when the sorcerer wasn't ready for him. The magician lost control of the situation when that happened, as his self-protecting defenses were down. And the magician's object was to keep the spirit in line, just where he wanted him, to do his bidding. If the spirit could get the upper hand, he would. (It could be psychologically debilitating for an all-powerful, all-being spirit to find himself imprisoned by, and forced to do work for, a mere mortal.)

Sorcerers also said a great many prayers. This is understandable, too. Faced with a spirit, or spirits, of unmitigated evil, who else was there, really, to turn to, for protection in an hour of need *but* God? So God was carefully and continually invoked to protect the magician, his instruments of magic, and his works against the nastiness of the evil spirits he conjured.

If you're going to indulge in the ceremony that I next set before you, a medieval sorcerer's method of causing death with a waxen figure, you must have a strong sense of historical curiosity. Be advised that you are going to need fortitude, patience, resourcefulness, clever hands, and, above all, a great deal of time. Either quit your job or save up your vacation days, because you'll need about two weeks to get your materials together, ready yourself, and then perform the feat. And unless you've had much experience with casting spells (successfully, I hasten to add) your foolhardiness would be extreme if you undertook the ceremony. But if you're ready for it, here's what you need to do. The instructions are taken from a rare family grimoire belonging to a sorcerer (he wishes to remain anonymous) who lives in Paris. I have made this translation from the French and, I hope, have made the process comprehensible.

First you need to make some shopping forays: to a department store for cloth, to a bookstore for a Bible (unless you own one), to your local occult herbalists, to a candlemaker, and to a bubbling brook in the country (among other places). Here are the items you require:

A large amount of red material to drape a room with
     (could be sheets dyed red)
A table to turn into an altar
1 Bible
1 length of red satin to be made into a robe
1 half-yard of black satin for making magical symbols
1 censer
1 aspergillum
1 large bag fresh coal
Myrrh
Red wine
A communion wafer (stolen from a church)
1 long pin with a ruby in it
Fresh spring water
2 black candles (with matches)
Virgin wax (made by you as a candlemaker does)
Cast-iron tongs (new)

Now, don't cheat on any of these items. You must find out how candles are made, for instance, by visiting a shop that makes them or by looking up the subject, then gather the ingredients and put together some wax for yourself. Melted-down candles just won't do. For all you know, their maker meant them to be used in a church, or at Thanksgiving dinner, or for a funeral, and his vibrations will adhere to the material and render it useless.

Now you're ready for the ordeal. Here are your first instructions:

Carefully clear out a room in your house or apartment and

clean it thoroughly. Now drape it entirely in red material (this means the floor and ceiling, too) and in the center of your room erect an altar and cover it also in red cloth. Now bring into your room an aspergillum and censer made of gold-colored metal (you can get censers at religious supply stores), some sanctified holy water, and myrrh for incense. For the next three days, while sitting in the nude in your room, give yourself over to reading the Bible and meditating. At dawn and dusk of each day, say the following prayer:

> Lord God of the Heavens,
> Look down on me
> And be merciful unto me
> Even though I am a sinner.
> I dedicate myself to You,
> Humble myself to Your awesome power,
> And pray for Your grace.
> Be compassionate, O Lord,
> To Your loving servant,
> And help him in this hour of need. Amen.

At midnight on the third day, drink red wine and eat a communion wafer (stolen from a church). As you sip and eat, say the following prayer:

> I take the benediction of these items, Oh Lord,
> That they may preserve me from any evil vapors and
> Hell creatures cast up in the course of my undertaking.

Then swing the censer (with myrrh burning in it) around the altar perfuming the area, and sprinkle the altar and your nude self with holy water. Say as you do the sprinkling:

> O Great Lord Adonay,
> Purify my body and this room,
> Even as this, the water of Your earth,
> Is holy, sacred unto You.
> Make me clean in body and
> Especially in soul,
> And make this temple sanctified,
> And full of Your presence. Amen.

Now it's time to ready your robes, which you'll only wear during the actual ceremony. Have on hand a length of red satin and sew it in the style of a tunic, reaching to the floor. Across the heart, sew in black satin a waning moon, two inches high. On the back, put a five-pointed star, also in black. When the garment is finished, take it into your room, lay it across the altar and swing the censer over it saying:

May this holy incense of God cleanse you, my robe,
Of any earthly soil
And of any being which would hide in your folds to destroy me.
I cast you out, filthy substances,
In the name of the Holy Trinity. Amen.

Now, taking up your aspergillum, sprinkle the dress while saying:

Sanctify, O Lord,
This robe so that its
Holiness will keep in abeyance
Any familiar that would try to
Touch me in the operation I am about to perform.
May this robe keep me safe from

Creeping evils, from flying manifestations,
And from the Lords of the Rings whom I do conjure.
Amen.

Now fold up your garment and lay it on the altar.

I've mentioned that you should be using myrrh and holy water in these various ceremonies of preparation, and the proper prayers to say over these items, to make them holy, follow.

Prayer to Say Over Incense

When you wish to use the myrrh, first put fresh coal in your censer, light it, and say this prayer:

Lord God above,
May the fire of this coal
Burn with a holy light and
Terrify the powers of the
Night forces that rise from the ground,
So their eyes turn away in fear. Amen.

Now add some myrrh, and as you cast it on the flame, say:

Sacred incense of God,
Carrying the scent of holy endeavors to Him,
Burn in this sacred flame,
And let all who breathe you
Fill with the presence of the Lord,
And let the wicked flee before your powerful odor,
And fall upon the threshold of God,
And melt away beneath His powerful light.
Cast out all black spirits, sacred incense,
From this chamber. Amen.

Whenever you finish using the censer, don't just put out the incense. Say as you do:

> Oh, most powerful Lord,
> I extinguish the fire of Your sacred perfume,
> But may You see fit to keep its holy and perfect
> Influence lingering here,
> Powerful against mine enemies. Amen.

To Make Holy Water

The one quality which holy water must possess above any other is purity. You simply can't take water out of your sink tap and think you've got the makings of good holy water. It's polluted (by chlorine, at best). Find a well out in the country, or a pure brook or a spring, but whatever you do, get the real thing. If you don't bother, you'll only sabotage yourself, because impure water is the favorite of devils. When you have your water, say this prayer over it:

> God Most Powerful,
> I take this earthly substance
> And dedicate it to You on high,
> That Your Spirit may flow into it
> And cause whoever is touched by it
> To partake of Your blessing.
> May it hold Your power, Your Word
> And Your benediction forever. Amen.

Now, whenever you want to use your holy water, carefully pour some in your aspergillum and say as you do:

> Most Blessed Father,
> Creator of the Heavens and Earth,
> May this holy water, which is
> Dedicated to You,

Keep back all manner of evil beings
And impure spirits who would enter here.
May it carry the
Power of Your Word, Oh Lord. Amen.

In the same spirit, when you finish using your holy water,
don't just empty it down a drain, but pour it back in the
container where you keep your supply while saying:

Oh Lord God Adonay,
As I take Your most holy water
Out of its sacred vessel,
I pray that You'll see fit to
Maintain its influence in this chamber,
And keep it safe from any evil being
Which might try to violate it.
Hear me, Oh Lord, I am Your servant. Amen.

It is also extraordinarily important to understand that the
actual ceremony that you will perform—making the waxen
doll—must be accomplished during the day and hour proper
for overthrowing enemies. It would never do to attempt to
kill an enemy during the time when love spells are potently
made. Therefore, here is a schedule of the hours of Mars
that are suitable for doing away with people:

Sunday: 7 a.m.,   2 p.m., 9 p.m.
Monday: 4 a.m., 11 a.m., 6 p.m.
Tuesday: 1 a.m.,   8 a.m., 3 p.m., 10 p.m.
Wednesday: 5 a.m., 12 p.m., 7 p.m.
Thursday: 2 a.m.,   9 a.m., 4 p.m., 11 p.m.
Friday: 6 a.m.,   1 p.m., 8 p.m.
Saturday: 3 a.m., 10 a.m., 5 p.m., 12 p.m.

Now, when you've selected the hour during which you
will proceed with your ceremony, take with you into your

room your pin with the ruby in it and the lump of wax
you've made to turn into a doll. Put these on the altar between two lighted black candles. (Don't forget to also bring
with you a pair of new cast-iron tongs with which to hold
your doll. The wax may harden before the image is complete, and you'll need to put it in a candle flame to resoften
it.)

Now don your red robe saying:

In the Name of the Father, the Son, and the Holy Ghost,
I do kneel before You (here kneel in front of the altar)
Oh mighty Spirit of Death,
And I do dedicate myself to Your work,
To the destruction of my enemy,
To the bringing down of thunder and lightning
To strike him dead.
May he perish and never see
The face of God or His Holy Angels. Amen.

As you knead the figure into shape, speak this incantation
over and over:

Come into this wax,
O Spirits of Darkness,
Mighty Lucifer, Bealzebuth,
Leviuthan, Balbirethe,
Asmodeus, Asteroth.
Materialize, I command You,
And fill this image with Your rage,
Fill it with Your sulphurous powers.
Take this image of (speak your enemy's name)
Which contains his Name, his soul,
And kill it, kill it,
Expend Your angers on it.
Kill [your enemy's name], I command You!

When you've finished your doll, lay it on the altar between the lighted candles and, taking up your pin with the ruby in it, pierce, with all your enmity, the heart of the image. Now remove your robe and go out of your chamber silently (let the candles on the altar burn out by themselves). At either dawn or dusk (whichever is closest after the ceremony) return to the chamber, put on your robe and, taking up your holy water, sprinkle the doll in the name of the Father, the Son, and the Holy Ghost. Light your censer and purify the chamber. Then go out (after removing your robe) and don't return till your enemy is dead. (Amen.)

If you really did go to all the trouble of doing the full-dress black magic ceremony, and have gotten your way—your enemy is murdered—it's possible that you're sitting around twiddling your thumbs or making cat's cradles and chortling about how clever you've been (oh, chortle, clever me!) and thinking what fun it is to have your own way. You're probably even projecting your success into the future and are ecstatic at the possibilities you see there for evil.

No more rich Aunt Agatha? In future, there may be no more wicked Uncle John and insufferable Cousin Hughie. You've always wanted your boss's job? Maybe there'll be no more boss, too. The ceremony is, of course, a heck of a lot of trouble to go to, and killing people is a bad bag to get into. But if you're naturally wicked . . .

Supposing all didn't go as you had planned, however. Maybe you got tired, after a bit, of reading the Bible and meditating on holy subjects, and goofed off. Maybe you thought you'd found a pin with a ruby in it, but it turned out to be glass. You were lost and didn't know it.

Meanwhile, there's your wax image lying on the altar—growing mold by now, for all you know—and nothing. Nothing's happened. There's your enemy, big as life, walking around the supermarket, stocking goodies for what looks like

the next ten years—oblivious.. Not a dent anywhere. Especially in the appetite. Failure.

By now you must have one hell of a headache—a finely
honed migraine—just pulsating you to death with every
heartbeat. Have hope—there's that, even now. Cast the following spell and transplant your headache to your enemy.
He should be suffering a *little*, don't you think? From the
peasants of France, here's how it goes:

Take the freshly laid egg of a black hen, still warm,
and hold it to your forehead while saying:

> Take away the pain,
> Take it away,
> Evil pain
> Into the egg go,
> Into the new one,
> Into the unhatched
> Go, you pain.
> Take the pain and
> Give it to my enemy.
> Let him eat the pain,
> Let him suffer,
> I give him my pain.

Now pay a little visit to your enemy and give him the
nice egg as a thoughtful gift for his morning repast.

Part III

AMULETS AND TALISMANS

CHAPTER VII

Functions of Amulets and Talismans

If you don't own a midi, a shawl, a shoulder bag, a jacket, or a pair of boots with fringe on them (seems impossible by now), go out and get yourself such an item. Not only will you be marvelously swingy in your fringes, you will have a great time wherever you wear them. Fringe completely protects the wearer from the malevolent influence of the evil eye. Bad spirits don't like fringe because it's too distracting to them, and they keep away. Ask any Arab camel driver and he'll tell you the same story. (Look carefully, and you'll notice that his camel's saddlebags have long fringes dangling from them.)

Incidentally, evil spirits hate tassels, too. Start a little fashion of your own with them—perhaps braiding them into your hair, or letting them hang in a passel from your hips. Need I remind anyone that strippers have *always* worn tassels, and that it might be amusing to take a cue from them and learn to swing a few of your own?

If you think I'm beginning to sound like a fashion magazine, it's because amulets and talismans are body adornments, often worn as much for their effect as jewelry as their magical properties. All that gorgeous Egyptian stuff you see in the museums? All those silver filigree necklaces and rings worn by the women of India? All those marvelous bone things you see on African chieftains and their ladies? Amulets. That's what they are, pure and simple. Just take bells, for example. Little clinky silvery bells found in Arabian anklets and bracelets. They're meant to keep away evil spirits. Church bells, too, have significance beyond calling the faithful to prayer, or announcing a marriage or death. They were originally used to keep back the evil ones. In modern caverns, beyond the fringe, look for bells—on horses, asses, camels, and their drivers.

An amulet's job is to protect the wearer from any kind of trouble. This trouble may come from evil spirits (such as those you've been rousing against your enemies), or from the evil eye. The eye of the human being is the focusing device of a very powerful force—the human mind when it's engaged in bewitching. People are forever projecting emotion at each other, and should you find yourself, for example, in the position of being generally envied over some good fortune, the powerful feeling spent on you as people congratulate you while thinking negative, jealous thoughts is bound to have an effect. Negative emotion sent your way can even sometimes reverse your luck and leave you wondering what you did to deserve this. Nothing. Sheer witchcraft at work, that's all.

I always wear an amulet. Since I've acquired it, I feel a thousand percènt better. There are a lot of heavy, bad vibrations in the air (like pollution), and an amulet nullifies their effects. I've been lighthearted (can't remember when I was last depressed), positive, and, strangely, nothing really bad seems to happen to me any more. Not a tear has crossed my cheek in six months (an all-time record). And if something ghastly should occur, it won't, I know, make me feel that the end of the world has finally come.

You acquire an amulet by discovering it. Maybe it's one

that's described in this next chapter, or maybe you see a bit of glass or a stone, perhaps a carving or a piece of jewelry, and you eye it. Oddly, it seems to eye you back. You just feel it saying to you, "Make me," or "Pick me up," or "Buy me," whatever. You get this powerfully good feeling from the object, as if it were possessed of a supernaturally strong protective power. Now don't go around keyed up trying to find your ultimate amulet. If you do, every bead and buckle is going to seem like one. Your desire for the good-luck charm will make you become so tense you'll lose your judgment about it.

It's essential to understand that you'll happen upon it. When you see it, you'll know that this is the amulet you need. I wasn't looking for one, nor had I ever thought of owning one when I stumbled across mine. Oh. When you find your piece, be prepared to face poverty. If your amulet happens to be something you see in a shop, no matter what the cost, your eyes will glaze over and you won't be able to make out your check for it fast enough. My advice: stay away from expensive places like Tiffany's, objets d'art stores that carry museum pieces, in fact any supercostly emporium. Could be a disaster. In debt for nineteen years.

Now a talisman has a slightly different function. Its protective influence covers one specific area. For example, if you've just moved into a super, top-floor apartment in a New York brownstone that has *everything*, including a skylight, you should probably make a talisman to keep away thieves. Skylights in top-floor apartments are an open invitation to addicts in search of goods to pawn. Your goods, in this case. Just hang a little decorative talisman above your front door, and relax. No one will bother you.

Or, as protection against the next stock market crash, you've decided to bury a fortune to see you through. No good just to put all those neatly stacked piles of money into the *earth*. Suppose your neighbor's dog rooted up the money and the neighbor's little boy decided it was great fun to watch the pretty green papers sail away on the breeze. Heaven forfend. Put a protective talisman with the money when you bury it, and no animal, be it four-footed or two, will find it.

In this chapter, you'll find a wide-ranging selection of amulets and talismans to make, as well as a discussion of the properties of various amuletic and talismanic stones. Some of the charms are so ancient they date back to the beginning of history. Others are contemporary. Whichever item speaks to you, make it up and watch your luck change for the better.

⋖§ Talisman for Air Travel §⋗

While I adore to travel and in fact am consumed with a desire to be off and away to the far corners of the earth, I must admit that I'm extremely wary of airplanes. I've flown a good deal in the last five years, and each time I board an aircraft I'm aware that the odds of my being involved in a crash are increasing. Not a happy thought as I mount the steps.

I've taken to trying to psych out airplanes. Sounds peculiar, I know, but I figure if I ever get some sort of ESP message about a plane, no matter how much trouble it is to change reservations and remove luggage, I'm *not* going anywhere on it. So I keep all the channels open when I look at planes.

Just because I get no particular vibration from a plane once I'm aboard doesn't mean that I relax and feel secure about the trip. No indeed. I settle in the seat and lean back in a most nonchalant way, but if anyone were to notice my knuckles, he'd see just how I feel about air travel. Someone once told me that the most dangerous moments in flying are at the takeoff and the landing. So I don't breathe when we zoom down the runway and never think "Well, that's over" until the "No Smoking" sign goes off. When the plane lands, it's the same story, only this time I add a little prayer of thanksgiving. (I've even been known to make wild, whispered promises to the Creator in mid-flight if He would only see to it that the plane arrives safely.)

I'm honestly not sure if pilots and stewardesses are mad or naive. If we feel vulnerable to crashes, what must their vulnerability be? Out of sympathy for all air travelers, but especially for airline employees, I offer this medieval talisman for travelers to promote safety off the ground. (It also promotes eloquence of oratory on the ground.) Have a gold disk inscribed with the following words: "Swiftly, Safely in the Eye of God," and wear it about your neck on a chain.

✑ Talisman to Protect Your Apartment ✐

There are some apartment buildings that seem to reek with bad vibrations. And in these days of scarce pads, it always seems as though the cheapest ones, the ones you actually can afford, are in buildings with the very worst auras. It's just not fair. You search and search, wear yourself down with looking, and when you actually come across a place and inspect it, you find that the atmosphere is so bad you just couldn't live there. Apartment hunting is a game of musical chairs, you decide, and you're the one who's always left over.

If you've really looked and can find no ideal abode, and the situation has reached desperate proportions—you'll be out on the street with your bed and dresser next week—then what you must do is make the best of it. Take that apartment that somehow turned you off—as long as it's not in an *area* that has bad vibrations, too—and set about removing the unsavory influences.

What you must do is go to a farm where there are horses

and casually scan the barn area until your eyes light on a discarded horseshoe. Check it out. If the nails are still in it, or lying close by, it's especially lucky (as the vibrations are still whole and effective). The horseshoe is an ancient good luck talisman, and when used properly it will ward off any evil that might try lurking in the door of your apartment. Its power derives from the moon, whose crescent it resembles.

The northern edge of the moon, the top of the crescent, is the luckiest part, as it symbolizes wealth and power. The southern exposure (when the tips are lying heavenward) symbolizes death, unhappiness, poverty. So, when you've acquired your horseshoe, take it home with you and find a nice spot over your new front door to hang it. Now don't forget: Nail it up so that the ends of the horseshoe are pointing downward. Don't let anybody tell you that when the points are up, your luck is caught within as in a cornucopia. This ridiculous rumor got started in our terrible, know-nothing age of magic.

⋙ Talisman to Make You Fleet-Footed ⋘

I'm always happiest, as I think most people are, when I have a day ahead of me in which there is absolutely nothing pressing to do. The laundry's done, the groceries are bought, the house is cleaned, nothing to do. How divine. Maybe a day at the beach would be just the thing. Or perhaps ten straight hours curled up in a chair reading by the fireplace on a wintry day. Or maybe a long walk, window-shopping, or, joy, strolling in the country. But days with nothing to do are rare jewels indeed.

Most of the time we schedule ourselves into fantastic binds. Rise at seven, out of the house by eight, pick up the laundry or go to the drugstore and be in the office by nine, work until noon, rush off to pick up a book, a new dress, or visit the dentist, get back to work until five, do the grocery shopping, fix dinner and maybe get ready for a date at eight, then fall into bed at two. Enough to kill a horse. You can't last very long on a schedule like that. And what has really been done? Drugstore, laundry? You have to be kidding.

Nevertheless, sometimes it's necessary to wreck ourselves to get the little things done. It would be so much more justifiable, though, if we were ruining ourselves writing a novel, or getting no sleep at all because of play rehearsals. But that's not the case.

When you're faced with one of those ugly, do-everything days and are determined to get all the little nasties over with at once and as quickly as possible, then treat yourself to a talisman that will help you get through it with a minimum of agony and loss of breath. Wear a chain with a bird in flight on it (made of silver or enameled in white), and your swiftness will amaze you.

◄§   Talisman for Business Success   §►

The most successful women I know in business are not only extremely bright and educated, but have driving ambitions that spring from a surprisingly similar source. They all, more or less, had insecure childhoods.

When they were little girls, these big-time achieving women were often the scapegoats. You know, the maybe-too-fat, or maybe-too-thin, girls who were shy and sensitive, and whose classmates, sensing their vulnerability, made fun of them and often teased them nearly to tears. When it was time for rope-skipping or hopscotch, the sensitive little girls were forever being told to go away, no one wants to play with them. When there was a roughhouse in the schoolyard, the sensitive little girls were the ones who were chased and pummeled by their classmates.

As these little girls grew, they had a very difficult time of it, for their egos were damaged. Their early experiences left them feeling inferior, and they regarded themselves as failures in just about every area. There isn't a parent in the world who, with love and care and understanding, can really heal a little girl who has been rejected by other children. (If her parents, on top of her other troubles, don't treat her lovingly, a sensitive child may become so emotionally damaged that she'll never recover.) She must make her way by herself, and try to renew her own sense of worth as best she can.

When she's made some sort of peace with herself, the sensitive young woman often becomes driven by the idea of success. She must be a success; she's never been one, and her ego requires it. And if she's bright, with a good education, chances are she makes her success happen—as a superachieving business woman. To help ensure success in business, have the Egyptian hieroglyph, which means "to be powerful" cast in gold, and wear it on a chain.

A magazine editor friend of mine had a most marvelous experience with this next talisman. Its power is remarkable indeed. She and a very well-known photographer had been assigned to do a story on one of the most famous political figures of our day. The politician had a close adviser who helped my editor friend make the proper arrangements for the interview and photographic sessions. They were to meet the politician at a ski resort, for they wanted to portray him in his most relaxed moments. Both the editor and the photographer ski, so they had plans to photograph him actually out on the trails.

All the arrangements seemed set. When the editor and photographer arrived at the ski resort, the first thing they did was to get in touch with the adviser. "What were your names again?" he asked. "Oh, I see. Yes, I remember something about this. Un-huh. Well, I'm afraid you can't photograph today. So-and-so is very busy right now and intends to go skiing shortly."

Nightmares are made of this stuff. And it happens all the time. Outraged, but playing it cool, the editor and photographer went around to the mountain where they thought the politician would be skiing, cameras and notebook in hand. And sure enough, he soon appeared. The editor is very attractive and knows how to wheedle her way with the best of them, so she went right over to the politician, introduced herself and the photographer, and explained how they had made appointments to interview and photograph him. Would it be a terrible imposition, though, to get started now and to take a few pictures here, while he was lacing up his ski boots? "Yes, it would be," the politician said, and stalked off.

With nothing further to be done, the editor and photographer returned to their lodgings. At this point, the editor donned her talisman. Later, back at the ski lodge where the politician was staying, the editor and photographer came across him having a drink in the bar. This time the politician rose to greet my friend, shook her hand, and invited her and the photographer to join him for a drink. He apologized for being rude and asked if he could meet them at nine the next morning for a shooting and interview session. He was charming, and they spent several hours together chitchatting about the world over hot toddies.

The talisman which my editor friend wore that night is of

African origin, and overcomes misunderstandings and quarrels in a business situation. It's the figure of a lion with a ball grasped in its teeth (have it made in gold).

There are a few boutiques in New York that really turn me on to shopping, as the selection of clothes is up-to-the-minute, witty, sophisticated, and beautiful. When I'm in one of those marvelous shops, I don't look at price tags (the clothes are invariably expensive). I simply heave a sigh and produce my Master Charge card. (What the expense account has done to the marvelous New York French restaurant, the Master Charge has done to the marvelous New York boutique—bandits' prices are *de rigueur* with shop-owners who know you can pay for a dress in ten-dollar installments.)

When I do my shopping routine, I begin at Contagious, which is on Third Avenue between Twenty-first and Twenty-second Streets. No one else has material such as can be found here in the sweeping evening pajamas and bikinis. Then I take a taxi to Ninth Street and walk east to It's on You, where all the models hang out for the wonderful leather things. Then I bus it to Fifty-third and walk over toward Second Avenue to Betsey, Bunky and Nini, my all-time favorite place. You can walk away with an Ossie Clark or a clingy something by Betsey Johnson, or almost best of all, a little Danish import for, sometimes, practically nothing, to wear to the office. Absolute heaven here. When you've bought your inexpensive little import, you can then splurge on a hand-painted belt at twice the figure.

My newest love, however, is The Sweet Shop, next to Betsey, Bunky and Nini, and Kamali (which has snake dresses and cock-feather chokers, incidentally). The English designer Laura Jamison has her clothes here, and they're irresistible. Buttery suedes, bazonnga crepes. Chiffon blouses that look like garden parties in the twenties. I got so excited when the shop first opened that I gave the manageress the following Egyptian symbols (which signify "dominion") to ensure business success. Write them on parchment, and wear on your person.

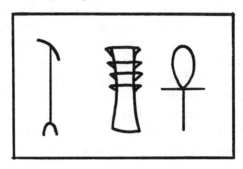

❧ *Talisman to Enlarge Your Intellect* ☙

It's particularly marvelous to be a woman right now if you want to work because all of the businesses are feeling sensitive about their nondiscriminatory stance. It's downright embarrassing to have a bunch of Women's Liberation ladies camping out on a company's doorstep waving nasty signs and making even nastier ones at the incoming and outgoing executives. Who needs that? Especially when the TV networks invariably set up shop next to the ladies and let them rap on for all the world to hear about what an ugly company they're picketing.

So upward mobility is now quite possible for bright, attractive women who have a yen to take over. The barriers in publishing are especially weak; I know several college graduates who have lept from secretary to editor in six months. And I have great sympathy for such young tycoons, as getting a marvelous job is one thing, but keeping it quite another. Hard on the nervous system.

For example, one presumably talented, very young girl moved into a job like mine. I have six years' experience that she doesn't, so my job seems rather simple-minded to me. To her, however, it has loomed large, very large indeed. She began to talk to herself, a little undercurrent of mumble that eventually grew into outright loud phrases. It took me quite a number of hours to figure out what was happening (she never admitted, of course, that she felt overwhelmed by it all). I really did try to calm her down in all the ways I could think of—subtle, of course, to preserve what was left of her ego—but she didn't seem capable of applying my soothing remarks to her situation. Once I said, "Oh, I hear you've been assigned one of those fun, easy-to-do research and writing projects." She just stared at me wide-eyed, fear oozing from her sebaceous glands. I really felt sorry, but what could I do?

Then I remembered the following talisman, which helps increase the intellectual capacity and assures ability in writing and public oratory. I told her about it, she had one made, and she's begun to relax. Molded in gold (or it may be engraved on a topaz) it is a sunburst with a coiled snake in the center.

◄§ Talisman to Keep off Fear of Ghosts §►

If you've got a vivid imagination and are inclined to be jumpy, then there's no hope for you. All your life (and you've just got to learn to live with it) you're going to be plagued with nervousness about apparitions—meeting them, that is.

Every time you go up into someone's attic, even your own, you'll open the door carefully and pause, just a moment, to be sure you detect no movement above. And as you rise with each step, you'll keep your ears cocked to pick up the tiniest shuffle, your senses alert to any odd breath of air. But chances are, you'll work it so that you won't have to enter an attic alone in the first place. Jumpy people spend a good deal of time protecting themselves against situations that will close their throats with fear.

It's the same situation when it comes to cellars. These can prove to be even more difficult, however, because cellars always have pipes and furnaces that make menacing creaks and sputters and hisses that just add to the general sense of uncertainty and terror you feel about descending to them. Here, you instinctively know, are perfect hideaways for ghosts, and you're sure that any you might encounter here would be dangerous—the kind that would definitely attack you.

Jumpy people rarely arrange their lives so that they have to live alone. Single jumpy girls have roommates, or lovers that live in. They would never admit it, but sudden, odd creaks in their apartments send them under the covers, and they constantly listen for footsteps in the other room. Their good sense tells them that if they live alone, they're vulnerable to ghosts suddenly seeping around door frames or sneaking up on them while their backs are turned in the kitchen or when they're in the bath washing their hair (on such occasions, they always lock the bathroom door).

If you face up to your fear of ghosts, then you can save yourself a lot of agony by having within reach a talisman to stave off that fear when you have a sudden attack of it. At such times, hold in your left hand a vanilla bean, and in your right a pinch of salt.

◄§ Talisman to Make a Judge Friendly §►

My great friend Douglas is in terrible trouble. He had, until recently, this marvelous Corvette (he now owns a staid VW), a real classic in which he sported about, turning girls' heads (he's excruciatingly handsome) and which, on occasions, he was known to drive rather fast.

Well, one night he was sporting along the throughway, and, nearing his turnoff, noticed a cop car pulled off to the side (the cop was handing out a ticket to some poor soul). So he slowed down (really far down, he says) and went on up the ramp. Then he heard a siren and, looking back, saw the cop car coming after him.

Douglas pulled over, thinking that the man was giving someone chase, and couldn't believe it when the car pulled up behind him. Well, something was happening with this particular cop, because he started swearing at Douglas and calling him things like punk, and two-bit you-know-what in a fancy sports car driving *under* the speed limit, and you guys all think you can get away with this kind of thing.

Ohhh, yesss. It's true. Poor Douglas—he really used to speed a lot, but not this time. The injustice of it all. Well, oh dear, he did say something rather gross to the cop. And of course he got a ticket and some awful threat about seeing him in court, and wow, what the judge was going to do to him.

But I hope I've helped him. Once I was in similar desperate circumstances and used this talisman for making a friend of a judge. Write on parchment, in two circles:

⮜ *Talisman to Overcome an Enemy's Hatred* ⮞

I've found that very few people in this world actually bear grudges for very long. Most people are kind of all right, and if you apologize for being rude and obnoxious and inconsiderate, they'll forgive you after a while. Not, however, my next-door neighbor. He's something else. (And, of course, oh royal pain in the neck, he *would* be my next-door neighbor.)

I invited my entire family to come visit me this year for Christmas and partake of my gourmet cooking (I can cook four great recipes successfully and they were staying four days) and general good cheer. Ha. My next-door neighbor, the night before they were to arrive, asked if he could borrow my *cookbook*, of all things. I was very nervous about his request and let him know that I was, but I said okay, he could borrow the book *if* he'd be sure to return it to me that evening. He didn't. Next day, only *hours* before I was descended upon, I tightly girdled my annoyance (no, it was anger, really), and went next door to retrieve the book. "Could I have my cookbook, please? I asked you to return it last night."

"Of course. I thought you would come and get it when you wanted it. You know my door is always unlocked."

"When I loan something, I don't expect to have to retrieve it myself."

That did it. His face flushed. I'd caught him in his manners. But he didn't blow up then; he let his fury seethe a while. When we next had occasion to clash, he screamed at me like a charwoman. Since that catharsis, he hasn't spoken to me. I've smiled at him on the street, in the hallway, in the supermarket (I really *have*). No response. He looks through me, around me, over my head. I know he'll never forgive me.

I really wouldn't care, except that I have a garden. My garden has grass. The grass is burgeoning, growing beyond my wildest dreams, green, tall. I need a lawnmower, and my neighbor has a lawnmower. I need to borrow his lawnmower and I can't. I've just had my jeweler run up, in gold, the following symbol (ancient Egyptian) to protect myself from enemies:

◄§   *Talisman to Protect Your Health*   §►

When the world gets too much with you, you're either the type of person who just gives it up, throws the towel in, lies down, and has a good cry, or you're the kind who increases your activity to the point where you become thoroughly confused. If you're the latter sort, you interest me. I'm not like you, so I watch your type. You're so busy keeping one appointment after the next that when you emerge onto the street from your office building, you turn left when you mean to go right, hail a bus instead of a cab, and are in a general state of total blitheringness.

If you only knew that there is really no need for all this confusion. There are reasonable ways to pace yourself. For example, the English have tea at four. Four is just about the time when one's morale takes a black turn downward. I know a very busy lady who, no matter what, and in whatever weather, simply takes herself out the door, down to the

street, and walks around the block at three-thirty every afternoon. I used to think she was nuts till I reached the state
of her busyness for just one week. Then I understood what
she meant.

When you're faced with what you know is going to be a
very hectic time—be it a week or a month, or even a lifetime
—do as the ancient witches recommended and carry about
with you a bit of wormwood. When you feel your stomach
churning about, your heart palpitating, your fear level rising, then take out your wormwood talisman and contemplate it.

But if you're past all calm and, in fact, are sure that you're
about to be victimized by a bleeding ulcer, then carry some
wormwood with a worm wrapped around it. As a talisman, it
is an antidote for stomach complaints of all kinds.

This past winter I was in Florida and the Caribbean doing
an article for the travel magazine *Venture* about the ultra-
chic goings-on at the new resort clubs. These clubs are
where a lot of very, very wealthy people hide out on winter
weekends, to escape the ugly weather in New York and the
annoying paparazzi of Internal Revenue agents and enemy
lawyers that constantly hound them. You come across Whit-
neys, Roosevelts, and Fords on sunny, palmy club terraces,
and can settle down for drinks (what a gas) with Joe Na-
math or Hugh O'Brien in the club bars.

Anyway, one night I was going to a charity fund-raising
dinner at The Palm Bay Club, which is the choicest one in
Miami. I had brought just the right dress, a pink satin Don-
ald Brooks, and I knew I would be *splendido*—in my element
at last. I was feeling absolutely marvelous by the time I
went up to dress, as I'd had some drinks and sparkling conversation with a stunning actor (who shall remain nameless;
I'm feeling coy) in the club bar and had been the center of
attraction. My attention was from a group of young, gorgeous socialites who spat hate darts at me, wondering who I

was and just how come I was having drinks with *their* play-thing (ah, the power of the magazine writer) while they tapped their long, polished fingernails alone, all alone, on the bar.

It may have been the hate they wished on me—a collective evil eye thing—because when I was ready for the bathtub, my stomach began doing a number. It groaned and creaked and finally did me in with the terrible Montezuma's Revenge. What a scene. Green, agonized, paralyzed, I lay on the bed. Thoughts of the party wafted round in my head. I cried, I actually did. When my stomach stopped thundering long enough for me to make it to the desk, here's what I did:

> On a piece of paper, which I then hung around my neck on a chain (always carry a chain with you when you travel) I wrote the following talisman:

> > Turn away evil eye,
> > Back to my enemy.

Now this is a very fine ancient Arabian remedy, and by the time I put on my gown I was ready to sail into the crowded party room, looking smashing and delectable. And that's just what I did.

❂ *Talisman to Maintain Hope* ₞

As I've said often, I don't especially advocate marriage. But a woman whose whole being wants it, whose very mission in life is to have a husband and children, is honestly doing her thing, and I admire her for it. I leave her to her fate; I let her alone. And I hope she finds the right man to marry.

The one girl I know who is the perfect wife type, punched from the pattern at a wife-type factory, is a Midwestern farm girl living in Chicago. (If a man wants a non-hassling, old-fashioned wife, he should immediately move to that city. Such girls are to be found there by the hundreds—it's a great gathering place for them, just as Greenwich Village is for heads.)

This particular girl came to New York to live, but was so completely overwhelmed by the gorgeously made-up and phony models and secretaries and struggling actresses that she went back to Chicago within two months. She had nothing whatever in common with the New York women who look forward to yacht voyages and Riviera vacations and weekends in the Caribbean with newly met rich men. Out of her element entirely. There was no one for her even to talk to. Her goals are a modest house, a husband with a moderate income, and children with good enough grades to get into the state university. Kind of difficult to talk about such simple hopes with a blonde dripping diamonds.

And then this wife-type *did* look awfully wifely. There was just no way that she could ever metamorphose into the kind of scintillating woman who acquires jewels. Kind of plump, cute, sweet—not sticky, however—just nice and open and friendly. Before she left New York, her ego was really down. She had lost all hope that she'd ever find the right man. The very thought of her without one made me shudder, so I gave her the following talisman, which preserves hope:

> Wear, pinned to your dress, a cluster of gold olives. You'll never give up.

৺§ *Talisman to Keep Away Scandal* ৡ৯

One of the wickedest things one human being can do to another is to start a rumor about him. And don't think that because life seems free and easy these days, with people's casual affairs hardly worth talking about and their financial misdemeanors virtually expected, a rousing scandal can't hurt one.

Just consider the case of poor Mandy Rice-Davies, who because of the Profumo affair in London some years ago lost her status as a party girl par excellence (what a bore for her, really). And the scandal that will always surround Ted Kennedy is a politician's nightmare come true.

It's practically impossible to hang around in the limelight and expect never to be the butt of a rumor. Even if your behavior is impeccable, people won't believe it, and will say nasty things about you anyway.

Just suppose you were at a party, as a well-known acquaintance of mine was recently, that was packed with celebrated and social figures from many realms. The hour was late (about three, she says) when the trouble began. One very drunk gentleman came rushing from a bedroom onto the crowded terrace wrapped in a sheet, which he dramatically threw open to expose his rather paunchy nude figure. Gay laughter all around. Several other men thought how fun, and divested themselves, too. By now the party was uproarious. The police came. The papers never put it quite as it was, but society buzzed for weeks about the event. What was so awful was that one of the exposed men was my acquaintance's date, and he thought it would be greatly amusing if she was nude, too. He managed to rip off her dress, bodice to hem, in his enthusiasm. Talk of her interesting body quite filled the grapevine for months. She hardly dared go out of the house.

If you would save yourself from slander, scandal, anything of that nature, make the following talisman and you will emerge unscathed:

Carry with you a little pouch of black satin in which you've put a pig's knuckle, a myrtle leaf, a white feather, and a bit of knotted black thread.

~ᴈ Talisman for Sexual Potency ᵹᴥ

Have you been languishing on your couch lately, the victim of general malaise, restless, unsure what to do about it? It may be that your trouble, if you think about it, comes from not having *felt* much of anything lately.

Have you been going to parties as usual, but haven't seen a man at any of them who seems interesting? When was the last time your heart did a flip-flop when a stranger, tall and good-looking, walked into a room? Is it just that there aren't any tall, good-looking strangers around any more, or is it that somehow you've gone and turned yourself off so you don't notice them? (Have you considered the possibility that you might be the victim of someone's witchcraft? Better think about it.)

If you've stopped feeling anything around men, you've probably also stopped feeling very much about anything. When your libido shuts down, so do you. You can be out in the sun sniffing cherry blossoms, but if your sexual feelings aren't operative, you might just as well be indoors reading a book. There will be no soul joy in the perfume of blossoms or in the tingly way the air ruffles the hair on the back of your neck. Your emotions won't thrill and set your blood rushing, making you high.

You should do something about your unhappy state right away. Seek out a man who goes hunting, and ask him to bring you the foot of a hare, if he shoots one. Then have the foot mounted, and wear it on a chain about your waist (next to your skin). The hare's foot is the protector talisman of sexual potency, and you certainly need it.

You might also consider making up the rather revolting but excellent potion to protect sexuality that I described in the aphrodisiacs chapter, and use that in conjunction with your talisman. Be careful, though, or you might turn on *too* much and find yourself scaling new heights up the walls.

↜ *Talisman to Acquire Wealth* ↝

Have you ever lived in a place where the bathtub is in the kitchen (and so unappetizingly marred with ground-in dirt and splatters of paint that you could hardly bring yourself to use it)? Do you know what it's like to live in a dingy room, gray with years of filth, that has bare bulbs and, for decoration, interestingly shaped holes torn in the walls? Have you ever heard the night movements of animals in the walls, or dreamed that a roach had crossed your lips in the dark and wakened to find it still sitting there? Have you ever crunched your way across a floor littered with dead bugs after you've sprayed, and had the light dawn that your neighbors don't spray for a very good reason?

Perhaps you've used your toaster, smelled something odd burning and, upon investigating, discovered a baby rat roasting in it. Maybe you've opened your stove and had a very large rat indeed scurry out. And maybe you've given up hope of ever controlling the wild life and the filth and the collapsing walls and the lightbulbs with bare wires exposed and the continual drip, drip, drip from the ceiling in the corner. A great many people live this way, you know. And have given up hope.

My contemporaries are down on money at the moment, especially those who have always had it and have no experience of slums. Money to them just isn't something to want any more—material amenities should be shunned. They say, just look around at the damage money does. People are living in boxlike houses with their cars and TVs and bits of lawn to tend on Sundays. They're all alike, living the same lives.

I believe that the people in poor ghettos lead identical lives, too. And I wish for them the comforts of those look-alike houses, with cars and TVs and lawns to tend and food to eat and even children to complain about it.

For people who wish for wealth, wear a talisman of seven gold rings on a gold chain, and it can be yours.

⊷§ Talisman to Fulfill Your Wishes §⊷

What is it that you want most in this world? Will your life be incomplete if you can't sail the seven seas and live in remote corners of the earth? Zanzibar? Tonga? Sumatra? Ceylon?

Would you perish if you couldn't, just once, know the passion of a man drowning in love for you, and feel yourself fully, completely, returning that passion?

Do you want a quiet life, far out in the country with a view of mountains and sea, where you can tend roses and nourish a field of daffodils in spring, and treasure the scent of lilies-of-the-valley in May?

Or could you be happy only in a Park Avenue penthouse with a rooftop garden and maids to serve you, where great paintings hang on the walls and rare antiques fill the rooms? Is your desire to dress in the Paris couture, relax in a beauty spa twice a year, and move about to your various houses every four months?

Could your private dream be to disappear to a Pacific island and never be heard of again? Would you love to have a Robinson Crusoe life with the sun and the peacock sea around you, as you reside in a grass shelter on the beach, swimming at dawn and fishing at noon? Nothing to do there but love a man and the jungle blooms, the tall palms, and salt-scented air.

There is a way to have your dream come true. A magic square, the Esaue, when properly used, will bring you whatever you ask of it. Write on parchment, with blood from your left hand, the following letters:

```
E S A U E
S        S
A        A
U        U
E S A U E
```

Visualize what you wish as you write the spell, and your dream will come true.

⋖§ *Talisman to Preserve Your Youth* §⋗

My own personal survey reveals that most men really don't know how to be in love. They're so busy protecting themselves from what they imagine to be the connivings of females who are, they think, only after their money or their bodies or both, that they very rarely let their hearts flower and feel the sensations of love. How very sad for most men.

True, women are rather intent on marrying. One girl puts it this way: "If I'm not married by the age of thirty, I'm really afraid people will think there's something wrong with me." She is being strictly honest. Too bad that women can't slay that dragon of "what other people think" once and for all. If more women did, there would be fewer fruitless marriages and, for both sexes, more delicious being in love.

You know how it is when a man first attracts you. Your heart turns over in your throat and your psyche tunes in to his every spoken and unspoken thought, his every desire. You become so excited by your discovery of him that you are compelled to let him know how you feel. You have to sit on your h̶a̶n̶d̶s̶ ̶t̶o keep from telling him you love him. When ̶y̶o̶u̶ ̶c̶a̶n̶ ̶s̶t̶a̶n̶d̶ it no longer and do tell him, chances are his ̶f̶a̶c̶e̶ ̶f̶a̶l̶l̶s̶ and he gets flustered. No matter that he might ̶f̶e̶e̶l̶ ̶t̶h̶e̶ ̶s̶a̶m̶e̶ ̶w̶ay about you. He just can't cope with being

̶T̶h̶e̶r̶e̶'̶s̶ ̶o̶n̶e̶ man I know who, when he falls in love, throws caution to the birds and lets his love just be, told me that he learned to be in love, vulnerable to it, by suffering a lot through love. He's been hurt often; instead of being bitter, however, he makes himself be open so he'll always be able to feel. He's beautiful, a man with the romance and passion of his early youth intact—a very rare creature indeed.

To help you always keep your youth, your vigor, and your heart, wear a talisman of sarsaparilla root on a chain next to your skin.

⊰ Amulets for Your General Well-Being ⊱

One of the most fascinating amuletic signs in the world is the swastika, not only because of its extremely long history (it has been found marked on artifacts of the Neolithic age), but because of its connection with the Third Reich. Let me point out immediately that there are two forms that the swastika can take, the life and the death. The life form looks like this: ⌐┤, and the death, an inverted form, looks like this: ┤┐ .

Hitler's infamous symbol was the death swastika. He could not have chosen a more appropriate symbol for his regime, as it turns out, because his death swastika is closely associated with black magic and is used in certain evil ceremonies. The black orgy of death he indulged in and his black swastika are cruelly, ironically, linked.

The life swastika, on the other hand, has the opposite connotation. It represents the essential hope and goodness of the human heart, the burgeoning of nature, renewal, spring. It is a truly venerable symbol for humanity, and has been used in every age. In the temple ruins of ancient civilizations in all parts of the world the swastika has been found. The ancient Orientals had it, and the peoples of the Fertile Crescent.

There are many people today who continue to use the swastika as an amulet. I personally can't wear it, because it offends my sense of the rightness of things. Hitler's black swastika is still too fresh a memory, and I wish to have nothing at all to do with the symbol in any form. Anyway, people don't make the distinction between the life and the death swastika, and I certainly couldn't bear to have even one individual think I was a Nazi.

If the life symbol doesn't bother you, it can be a powerfully good luck charm. If you have any reservations about its connotation, though, don't use it. Your mind possesses the ability to invert good vibrations and turn them bad, against you.

There are several levels on which you can involve yourself in the contemporary urban witchcraft scene. First, there is the no-involvement-at-all level—my favorite—which allows you complete mobility and a free hand in the selection of your friends. You can get into your witchcraft whenever you please (no cooling your heels, waiting for the coven to gather in somebody's dank basement) and wherever you please (basements are never very nice to work in, in the first place) and, best of all, you can get out of your witchcraft thing and lead a perfectly normal life when you feel like it. (If you don't go around telling everyone you know that you're into witchcraft, that is. People will bore you to death otherwise, with questions, questions.)

The second level of involvement is actually getting in with a small group of witches. This is okay if you're very sociable and are the sort of person who is fond of attending meetings, organizing refreshments—that sort of thing. If you think *your* group won't be like that, forget it. Somebody always wants coffee, and then somebody else thinks that's a nice idea and they'd like it with milk, please, and, oh yes, the hunger pains, how about a nice juicy hero sandwich? Pretty soon you're on your way down to the corner coffee shop with a voluminous takeout order to fill.

The third level of involvement is actually getting into the whole occult scene in your area. This means you know everyone who is anyone in it, and you're forever going out and doing things with these people. You don't know anyone who isn't in the scene, too (if you did, you couldn't see them, anyway, as all your social hours are spent being part of the scene). This level is the most dangerous one, as who knows what sort of mindblown freaks lurk at the fringe edges of the movement? Psychopathic murderers have been known, after all, to use witchcraft as an excuse to fulfill their sick needs.

No matter what level you're operating on, be sure always to wear the cross amulet. It's one of mankind's oldest, and its way with devils (which tremble in its presence) will keep you safe in an hour of need.

About a week ago, life became such a painful burden (what a shame for one so young and beautiful, you say) that I had to resort to my most powerful good luck remedy—the one I trot out for the most desperate circumstances. And they were bad. My younger brother and his wife are having their first baby soon, and they've bought a lovely new house, so my family decided it was time to grill me seriously about my own plans in this direction. You figure that once you're married, everyone will keep quiet and mind his own business, since your conventionality has now been firmly established. But it doesn't end here. Nosiness and harassment proceed unto the first child, and unto the second, for all I know.

And then other weighty troubles quickly developed. Suddenly our apartment, which is a sublet from friends, became unavailable. They returned from an unhappy sojourn abroad and needed it back. All that packing and unpacking of pots and pans again. And then my health began to fail. I was positive I'd been bewitched. My husband, too. He's been in a foul humor lately.

So out came my good luck antidote. The ingredients took me weeks to collect, but the time and expense were worth it. This amulet reverses all bitter attacks of fortune.

Put into a little white bag the following materials (wear the bag on a chain about your neck): one eye of a pheasant (put your order in with your local animal-stuffing establishments); one white feather (ask a chicken farmer if he'll save you some of these—it's best to have a supply on hand, anyway); a golden coin; a piece of coal; a fragment of rock crystal (small boys with rock collections always have at least one piece of rock crystal); some dust from a church altar (I got mine at St. Patrick's Cathedral). Your bad luck should soon change, as mine did.

One of the witches I hang about with in New York has for a secretary a most amazing girl. Gail. She's a millionairess, but absolutely real—a rare combination indeed. Well, my witch friend didn't really know much about the financial thing until the time that her secretary's sister called up for some advice. It seems that Gail's birthday was coming up, and since Gail had feted *her* with a surprise party for two hundred and had hired a rock group, she wanted to do something as splendiferous in return.

My witch friend suggested a surprise party, too, held to make it more surprising, four days after her birthday. That idea immediately won points, so the sister said she'd let my friend know in a day or two if the party was definitely on. It most certainly was.

It was indescribable. The sister lives, for a start, in a co-op apartment on Sutton Place. Right? She's twenty-two and owns a co-op. On Sutton Place. The party was for fifty, and included a catered, sitdown dinner. A battery of Chinese waiters served the meal. After dinner, Gail began opening her packages. When she removed the lid from the largest one, out popped her brother, who had flown in from Denver especially for the event.

All evening, everyone had been admiring a spectacular poster arranged in one of the doorways. A mighty rip, and through the poster stepped Gail's long-lost college roommate who is now married and living in Alabama. (Flown in, at the sister's expense, of course, for the occasion.) There was a great rock group to dance to, and endless champagne.

My witch friend, anticipating some sort of display, but hardly this, had been wondering what to give Gail as a birthday gift. It turns out her present was exactly right. A bouquet of pussy willows, when given to someone, assures them luck—a traditional token among English peasants.

If you should ever find yourself anticipating a trek about the back country of the Philippines, remember this warning: Keep your eyes peeled for various exotic forms of life that grow rampant in these islands. Take all of your most potent amulets with you for protection, or you may suffer the experiences of a reporter I met who spent several months there.

His first night out, miles from the civilized pleasures of Manila on the island of Luzon, he stayed in a wee hotel (more like someone's house where boarders were welcome). He was just finishing his unpacking and was preparing for dinner, when he glanced out his open window to view the dusky tropical light of evening fading among the flowering trees. "Aha," he told me he thought to himself, "I know that tree moved. I simply can't be crazy; I know that palm trunk undulated."

Nothing would do till his curiosity was satisfied—you know, new country, enormous curiosity. Downstairs and outside he went. He estimated where the palm would be, as seen from his window, then went right up to it. As his eyes adjusted to the heavy shadows, he became aware that he was staring eyeball to eyeball at the most gigantic green snake he had ever seen.

He says the prickles began on his forehead, moved to his armpits, and worked down to his feet. Sweat bubbled from his pores. He's quite sure he didn't utter "Yikes!" He thinks he took two steps backward, turned, and walked calmly back to his room. He knows that he lay down on his bed because the next thing he remembers was being eyeball to eyeball with the weirdest, most enormous spider he had ever seen—which had quietly lowered itself over his pillow and was just hanging there, swinging back and forth above his forehead. When he had successfully maneuvered sideways out of its path, and rolled off the bed, he discovered, on all fours, that he was even then eyeball to eyeball with the spider's weird mate. This time, the reporter admitted, he did scream. He rushed downstairs to the dining room, where he nervously described his encounters. Everyone laughed, of course. He never did recover from the Philippines, he says, and, indeed, he nearly leaped across the room when I later tapped him on the shoulder to give him a fresh drink.

To ward off all sorts of horrors, both at home and abroad, assure yourself the complete protection of the following amulet. Wear the Egyptian Eye of Horus, which, as a hieroglyph, literally means "Whole, sound, prosperous."

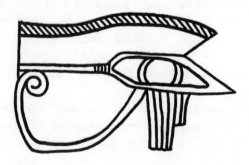

Never has there been a generation of human beings that has managed to do so much, and be in so many places, with such invisible resources, as the current one. I know more people, with apparently no money, who constantly crisscross the country, even the oceans, in search of fun. Sybarites, all of them. I secretly suspect they deal in drugs or, almost as bad, clip coupons or take money from their families. How else do they arrive in Zamboango? Not *everyone's* an accomplished stowaway.

Naturally, I brim with jealousy. Here I'm striving for the easy life—saving my money in piggy banks, scrounging whatever is scroungeable rather than spend a penny—and *still* far-out travel is beyond my reach. Meanwhile, broke friends (attired, mind you, in suede pants and jackets and other luxuries) are living the full, peripatetic existence my ideal easy life would be. And they don't work from nine to five. They don't work, period. They simply come and go as they please.

But they plan. Instead of letting details overwhelm them, they simply put their plans to work the way one friend did, subletting his apartment, hitchhiking to California, then scrounging a ride on an empty corporation plane on its way back to Japan. So how much money do you really need? Fifty dollars, in case you accidentally neglect, every now and then, to find someone to feed you? Easy coming and going obviously requires an adventuresome spirit. But it also requires good luck. To keep away the bad kind wherever you roam, consider wearing the following Yugoslavian amulet, which is made of metal and is six stars in a circulet, with three more in a triangle, set in the center.

Have you ever known people who seem to be hounded by misfortune on the scale of the classic Greek tragedies? I mean, besides the Kennedys. Something ghastly is forever happening to such people, and the events seem always to be beyond human control.

I've just heard about a family that has had so many inconceivable things happen to it that one is almost driven to believe in karma—what other reason could there be for such nonstop, lifelong horror?

The first mishap was the result of the son's and daughter's having an incestuous love affair. When the girl was fifteen, she gave birth to twins. Both of them died.

Then one summer night, the son was driving on a throughway with some friends. The driver lost control of the car; it plowed through the center guardrail and collided head-on with two oncoming cars. No one was hurt except the son, who was burned alive in the holocaust.

Several years later, the daughter went to waken her father from his afternoon nap and discovered that he had committed suicide. The trauma was overwhelming, and she began to lose her mind.

Meanwhile, the girl's mother had taken to drink and lost her sanity. Before the girl left home to come to New York, she had her mother placed in an institution, where she remains to this day.

In New York, the girl, mentally weakened by her family's tragedies, found the drug scene and moved in on it with a vengeance. She's a beautiful girl (perhaps *was*, by now), and may be found soliciting on the streets of Harlem.

To keep away any evils that might befall you (in the form of sickness or malevolent spirits), recite, regularly, this Hebrew formula (which may also be made into an amulet):

Abyar Abyar Abyar Abyar Abyar Abyar Abyar Abyar Abyar
Haga Haga Haga Haga Haga Haga Haga Haga Haga
Ye Ye Ye Ye Ye Ye Ye Ye Ye
Â Â Â Â Â Â Â Â Â

When I moved to New York, my health immediately went downhill. I'm not alone with this complaint, because practically everyone I know on first arriving in the city suffered the same symptoms.

Tired skin. You can't imagine how off-putting tired skin can be. You're afraid people will look at you, so you swathe your head in scarves and wear very dark shades and a lot of makeup. The trouble with the makeup is that it turns orange in the pores by three in the afternoon, and your tired skin then looks positively dead. Big sunglasses leave heavy dents across your nose that last forever. Scarves turn your hair oily in two days. What a mess. But tired skin is the affliction of all New York girls in the first year. It comes from staying out until three and four in the morning four nights a week and trying to maintain a nine-to-five job where you're scolded if you come in at five past nine. It also comes from poor eating.

I almost killed myself once with poor eating. I was a total psychological wreck, unable to function at all as a normal human being. I was living alone and going starkers. For six months, every night that I was home I compulsively tossed a chicken pie in the oven and had it for dinner. Can you imagine, chicken pies for six months? I guess at the time I thought they were square meals—you know, meat, starch, and vegetables (there is always a pea or two floating in the chicken gravy). I was also on a hot fudge sundae binge. At least three nights a week I'd have a hot fudge sundae. The corner Primeburger made hundreds off of me.

Life in New York is so utterly unlike life anywhere else (exciting, rushed) that it takes rather a long time for some girls to come to grips with its pace and find a proper, complementing rhythm that works for living in it. After all, we're not built to work all day, then attend every New York theater first night, every movie, every gallery opening, every new bar that's chic, within the first few moments that it's open.

Too much to do and see at once. The health fails. Tired skin takes over.

If you really must come to New York to live, my advice is to take a pile of vitamins every single day and try, somehow, to eat properly. Sleep will be out of the question for the first year. I also advise wearing as an amulet the Egyptian hieroglyphic which means "life, prosperity, and health." Have it etched on a square of gold and wear the charm about your neck.

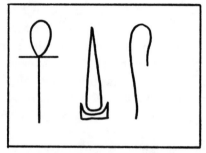

I've never been one of those extremely lucky people that we've all met who simply go through life having marvelous things happen to them—sometimes to the degree that they take their luck for granted. Such people never have their baked potatoes explode in the oven or get splashed by a limousine passing in the rain, and, worse, they never have broken hearts because they're so lucky lovers never leave them. If a relationship ends with a lucky person, it's the lucky person who ends it.

No. I've never had that kind of good fortune. Sour grapes, that's me. If I meet someone so lucky that it's positively painful, I immediately deem that individual to be unreal, not here at all, and, almost certainly, a positive phony. I begin to hunt for the flaws.

I think I've found the big one. I've studied so many really lucky-seeming people that I'm almost positive I've uncovered their secret. It's absolutely simpleminded: I think they

delude themselves. They *aren't* real. They imagine themselves (as in "have an image of themselves") to be lucky, so
when bad things happen, their minds discount them.

For instance, one girl swore to me that she'd never had an
affair with a man who, in the end, gave her the gate. So I
made her recount the history of her love affairs, and sure
enough, when she told me about two of them she wasn't bell-
clear on the course they had run. I pinned her down. Well,
in one case the guy told her he was leaving for Europe and
couldn't see her again. "Did he actually go to Europe?" I
asked. "Well, I don't know, I never pursued it," she answered. Aha! And the other one was an actor who got involved in his part in a play and couldn't see her any more.
Just as I thought. She just wasn't admitting to herself that
these men really broke up with her. Lucky people aren't
always lucky, they just don't admit bad luck when they have
it.

If you're a luck nut, you'll love this ancient Egyptian
hieroglyph and amuletic symbol to preserve the goodness
and beauty in your life. Made of gold, and usually strung in
numbers on a necklace, it's called the Nefer.

The evil eye is just the devil to contend with. You can be
in your office, minding your own business, when some girl
will come up to you and say, "Oh, what a pretty new dress
you have on." Only she's not just saying that. She covets
your dress. She's adding in her head, "and I want that dress,

but you have it, you witch. How dare you, a true frump like you, own that dress which *I* should be wearing in all my splendid beauty. But you, ugh. It looks ugly." She's put the evil eye on you because, while she's flattering you, the rays from her eyeballs are malicious. When you go out to lunch, you will probably spill coffee in your lap.

And, more deadly, you can be in a bar having a quiet drink with your lovely new man. Just sitting there, talking and sipping, being charming. And then you look up. There's this blonde next to you and she's been eyeballing him over your shoulder, and as you glance at her she smiles sweetly. Only the rays are horrible. Hate, hate. "How come you, a really ordinary-looking woman, are having drinks with that beautiful man who should be mine, all mine?" Don't get up to make a telephone call or go to the ladies' room. He'll be permanently engrossed with her when you come back.

There are a number of ways—endless ways, in fact—to deal with the evil eye. You can actually face the evil-eyer down, if you're brave, and say, "No. You do think this dress is lovely, but you think it's ridiculous on me. Just go away." The enemy will think you're a paranoiac nut (or, secretly, psychic) and probably say you're crazy, but the spell will be broken. You can also do things like drop your drink in the nasty blonde's lap and send her scurrying. But the only sure way to ward off the continual stream of evil eyes that besiege us every day is to wear an amulet as generalized protection. The Egyptian hieroglyph, the Shen, represents the all-powerful and conquering sun, and as an amulet is usually made of carnelian.

There's nothing like the sudden blooming of good weather in May to make you feel like you want to let out a whoop and run in the day for ever and ever. If you're doomed to four walls in a dark apartment, frustration can be total. So when the first hot morning dawns, get yourself out of there. Call a friend or a lover, but get a car and leave for the open spaces where there are fields of fresh grass and a bounty of soft, puffy, wafty clean air.

Once you've frolicked about in your chosen field a bit, settle down and feast on fried chicken and wine, or caviar and vodka, and the smile on your man's face (you did bring a lover, not a friend, I trust). And when you tire of eating, and are just lying there under the sun, stuffed and happy, run your fingers over the grass around you and play "look for the four-leaf clover."

Everyone is familiar with the good fortune that a four-leaf clover brings, but few people realize that it's even luckier to find one with more than four leaves. If you do come across such a clover, here, in meaning, is how the leaves line up. Starting at the left of the stalk:

The first leaf means happiness.
The second leaf brings health.
The third leaf indicates wealth.
The fourth leaf means love.
If you find a clover with more than four leaves, then:
A fifth leaf assures long life.
A sixth leaf means riches beyond counting.
A seventh leaf means you'll always be happy.

If you find one with seven leaves, you deserve to be happy forever after.

CHAPTER VIII

Amulet and Talisman Stones: What They Do

The wearing of amuletic and talismanic rings is an ancient practice, and it continues, undaunted, today. Many of New York's important jewelers have taken to selling rings of gold with zodiac symbols mounted on them, even, I note, made like the ones fashioned in the late nineteenth century for European ladies of chic and wealth.

Oriental peoples still wear seal rings both for the making of signatures on contracts and such, and as amulets. The metals and stones for seal rings are always carefully chosen for their owners by astrologers to invoke properly friendly influences.

In medieval Europe, wearing rings set with magical stones was widely popular. Also important were rings inscribed with little sayings, and our modern ring customs grew from those early traditions. Wedding bands, for example, are probably the descendants of ancient English rings used for a similar purpose.

There's been quite a history to the actual finger on which rings were thought to be suitably worn, too. In ancient times, amulet or talisman rings were usually put on the little finger. Later all this changed, and everyone began wearing rings on the first finger. Still later, people changed their minds again, and put their rings back on their little fingers. This happened because someone spread a rumor that there was a nerve in the littlest digit that ran straight to the heart. At the same time, wedding rings were placed on the regulation third finger (someone, sometime, also started a rumor about this finger, as we now popularly believe that it has a mystical connection with the heart). If you look at paintings of ladies from the sixteenth century, you'll note that they're wearing rings on their thumbs: these are amulet rings. Then the court ladies threw caution to the winds and, just as we did a year or so ago, wore ten or more rings all over their hands.

What has always remained constant is the significance of the stones used in making the amulet and talisman rings. A description of what particular stones do, follows.

◄§ For the Evil Eye §►

More than any other amuletic stone, I stand by the turquoise for all-around efficiency and efficacy. My own personal amulet, which I wear at all times (except to bed, where I feel reasonably safe from the unkind assaults of fortune) is a lovely, huge chunk of bright blue-green turquoise, the color of the Caribbean. It is surrounded by a large silvery metal hand-worked setting, and hangs from a chain. (It is rather heavy, and I shall probably be a hunchback by the time I'm thirty.) It comes from Rajasthan in India, where they understand amulets.

The traditional virtues of the turquoise are multitudinous. There is a legend that whoever wears one is invincible in the presence of wild animals. It seems an animal's attention becomes fixed on the stone and he's soon hypnotized (the amulet's wearer can then make his escape). It is supposed to protect the wearer from venomous bites (not much of a hazard in New York, but don't laugh off this virtue as you might have occasion to get stuck in the great desert snake country of Arizona).

The turquoise also protects its wearer from poisoned drinks and food. If you've been wondering why people in the old days were so concerned about poison that they needed amuletic protection against it, just cast your thoughts back to the Borgias; poison rings were so popular then and later that almost every antique shop today has at least one in stock. Also, if you were a medieval hag, you wouldn't have had much of a reputation in your community if you weren't familiar with poisons and methods of administering them. Today, poison isn't so important. Nevertheless, if you're into the witchcraft scene, you can't be too careful.

Another virtue of the turquoise is that it protects the wearer from blindness (good for contact-lens wearers who aren't so certain that this peril won't overtake them after twenty-five years of wearing the things). Arabs wear the stone to keep off the evil eye, and also for general good luck. It's even said that a turquoise amulet warns its wearer of impending bad health by changing color. I wear my turquoise simply to bring me luck, to keep off any nasty, evil vibrations that might be after me, and to protect my sanity which is more than enough for any one amulet to do.

✌§ For Evil Men §✌

While some women seem to attract almost exclusively ugly men, or the reverse, handsome men, others fall constant prey to evil men. The tricky part about evil men is that you never realize that they are until it's too late. At least with an ugly or handsome man, you know what you're getting into. Even namby-pamby men look like what they are—their jaws are slack, or their complexions are gray, or *something*. But an evil man doesn't have even a wicked gleam in his eye.

An evil man is one who tells a woman how much he loves and needs her, when all the time he really doesn't at all. He's just getting her to fall for him so that she will be in his power and lend him her money (which she never sees again), do his laundry and mending when she could be out enjoying herself flying a kite in the park, and do his cooking, which is slave work of the first order (all those hot stoves). What this evil man is really up to is getting some help cheap. He can't, or won't, afford a maid.

Chances are the woman in love doesn't discover the evilness of her man (they're always marvelous actors) until he decides he doesn't like her cooking or finds that she's not such a thorough housekeeper, or, indeed, is lousy about budgets. When she, stunned, wonders aloud to him why he's kicking her out into the cold, cold street, he will tell her exactly why. That's when she learns she's been consorting with an evil man.

Traditionally, a diamond keeps its wearer morally strong against any fleshly temptations which might beset her. A diamond also protects against fascination and drives off evil spirits and insanity. But, best of all, if a girl wears a diamond as an amulet on her left ankle, she will never be the victim of an unscrupulous man or, for that matter, any other con artist.

◄§ *For Danger* §►

Accident-prone prople really do have a hard time in this life. It's bad enough just coping with the traumas of daily living in a big city, but if you're accident-prone, you have your work cut out for you. Danger lurks everywhere: cracks in the pavement, treacherous curbstones, slippery streets. And if you have no sense of the rhythms in traffic—both street and sidewalk—you're really in trouble. Your ear doesn't pick out the off-key sound of movement that implies a taxi is about to carom around the corner into the crosswalk where you're about to step.

I knew a travel editor once who had just the worst luck with accidents. She was going on a trip to the Caribbean, and as she was walking up the steps to enter the plane, her heel caught in her hem, and she tumbled to the tarmac. Broke her leg—hobbled about on crutches and canes for months. The next trip she was assigned to was a lovely one to Egypt. Fell off a camel and broke her arm. That's not the end of it. She was the only traveler on the inaugural sail of the *Queen Elizabeth II* who had to go about with a bandage on her head. Seems she uninhibitedly dived into the shallow end of the pool.

My own single experience with being accident-prone leads me to believe that there's a lot of the power of suggestion at work here. I was trekking about up in Maine once, riding with some people in the back of a truck. The truck had a single metal bar, about head height, over which a canvas top could be drawn. The first thing one of my companions did, of course, was almost knock himself cold when he stood up to admire the view. We all admonished each other to remember the bar, but not an hour later I did the very same dumb thing. The only reason I can think of for my stupidity is that the power of suggestion drew me into its ugly trap.

If you feel yourself in constant danger from yourself, choose a talisman of mica and carry it in your pocket. When danger approaches, it will give you a prick if you put your hand on it.

For Cowardice

It isn't terribly difficult to identify a cowardly man. The demarkation point between "discretion is the better part of valor" and refusal to defend honor is perfectly clear. If you're with a date and a man passing by on the street comes close to you and snatches your shoulder bag, and your date just stands there looking sheepish and saying "Oh, dear," I wouldn't go out with him again, if I were you. Who needs a dumb man like that?

Or if you're with a date in a bar, having a friendly tot, and some drunkard comes over and starts slobbering at you because he thinks you're the most gorgeous creature he's ever laid eyes on, and his breath is reeking all over your hair (downright obnoxious creep), and your date just sits there nodding and smiling and doesn't take that nasty man by the elbow and help him toward the door . . . I certainly wouldn't want to see that date again. Suppose someone tried to snatch your purse on the street?

But it's much more difficult to identify a cowardly woman. What constitutes such a being? Women don't *have* to defend themselves physically from unpleasant types. Their *men* do it for them (though these days it does seem wise to take a course in karate). Cowardice in a woman is a much more subtle failing. I guess you would have to call a woman cowardly (just as you would a man) if she doesn't stand up for herself, speak up, if she comes under verbal attack. Or I guess a woman with ten children (or just one) who can't cope with all that responsibility and leaves them to fend for themselves might rightly be considered cowardly. If she were brave, she'd get some sort of help—either mental, or in the form of a nursemaid. To protect yourself from terrible moments of inward fear and quaking, wear a talisman made with a cat's-eye. (Incidentally, if you concentrate on an enemy while holding a cat's-eye in your left hand, you can put the evil eye on him.)

❧ *For Making Trouble* ❧

If you're timid and can't stand unpleasantness of any kind, especially open confrontations initiated by you with people you know well, then this next talisman is just what you need.

Suppose you've had a roommate for a year or so, and for the third time—which is once too often—she's ruined your plans. You invited your love over for a home-cooked dinner, and because your roommate didn't have anything to do, you kindly invited her to eat with you, too. Just dandy. You warned her, "Just you, though, nobody else," remembering the last time you were thoughtful, and she brought along Susie and Joanie and you wound up cooking for five people. You hadn't dreamed, then, that she would do such a thing, especially after the uproar (or was it?) you made when it happened the first time. Tonight, just as you were going to set the table for three, your roommate telephoned and said she was bringing Roxanne. "You can't *really* mind, can you? I mean, after all, you've got a *date* and I'll have no one to talk to after dinner."

This inconsiderate roommate has thus caused you to make an extra trip to the grocery store—practically at zero hour— and to take on the added expense of another steak, Idaho potato, and more tomatoes for the salad. Just who does she think you are? Jackie Onassis, who can finance the feeding of an army? A highly paid cook who doesn't mind a steamy kitchen? All you wanted to do was look pretty when your love arrived, and be organized enough to feed him in relatively short order. After a drink.

So now you decide that your roommate must go. No more hassling for you—out, out, *out*. But painlessly. Just get her a talisman (say it's for good luck—it is, for you) made with black onyx, and she'll soon be packing. Black onyx is an infallably unlucky stone when given as a gift. Your room-mate's surrounding vibrations will become so unpleasant that she'll simply pack up and move on (taking the bad vibrations with her, of course, but that's not your concern).

✑ For Causing Rain ঽ▹

Nature every now and then loses its grip and perpetrates what we like to call "acts of God" against us. Thus we have avalanches that sweep away whole towns in a mighty roar, forest fires that indiscriminately rage out of control to devastate communities, and gigantic floods and winds that level sections of the countryside in a sweeping swath. What, we wonder at such times, has possessed the powers above to wreak such havoc? If only the elements could be controlled.

Like our earliest ancestors, we still somehow feel that there is a superpower which is responsible for natural disasters. We sense a vindictiveness in nature that seems almost human in its malevolence. Indeed, we sometimes get paranoic about the weather.

Have you ever planned a fancy picnic to entertain a beautiful new man in your life, and then had to call it off because of the rain—not the dribbly kind that usually ends at noon, but the heavy downpour type that lasts all day? Makes you think that the Fates are, indeed, hags. Or what about the winter ski weekend you saved all summer for, even planned your vacation around? The weather was balmy, wasn't it—turned the packed snow to sheet ice so you could hardly walk, let alone ski. I know for certain that if I get my hair done, it's going to rain that day. Or if I'm going to a formal gathering, the wind will gust and throw grit in my carefully made-up face.

Magicians have been controlling the weather forever. Rainmakers and rain dances are proverbial. And I put more faith in them than in our modern cloud-seeding techniques.

The talisman stone of magicians, in many present-day tribes of the Pacific islands, which invariably attracts rain is lava. If your very worst enemy is planning an outdoor party on a Sunday, carry a bit of lava in your palm that day and think rain.

⊷§ *For the Sun* §⊷

It was one of those silent, motionless summer days in the Bahamas, when the sun dawns blazing out of the sea and seethes white-hot till the humid darkness finally moves in a breeze. We had risen with the sun in Nassau, and were now, a short flight later, on Andros, one of the untouched Bahama out islands, full of mangrove swamps and jungly under-growth.

There were three of us, and we hired a boat with a sturdy outboard motor and a likely looking lad for a captain, and set out to circle the island in search of an idyllic beach on which to pass the day.

We lazed our way along the coast, stopping now and then to fish, now and then to swim, and were perhaps an hour from the nearest settlement, when the motor suddenly ex-ploded into flames. The sheets of flame so startled us that we didn't realize for a half-minute or so that we might be in danger (if the gas tank had caught, we could have been blown out of the water). The young helmsman produced a fire extinguisher, but was in such a panic that he couldn't figure out how to work it. One of the men grabbed it away from him, pulled the proper ring, and as quickly as the fire had started, it was out.

With much relief, we rowed ashore and beached the boat. Only then did we think how far we might be from a town. Very far, we proved to be.

It was like some scene out of *The African Queen*. We waded through endless swamp, a foot deep in muck (I didn't dare look down to see what wildlife might be lurking about my toes), and crossed a rushing, precarious stream (close your eyes, take a deep breath, quickly peek at your next foothold, then *go*). The biting bugs were fierce. The sun burned down, boring into us, putting us, finally, into a trance. When we reached civilization, everyone had sun-stroke—except me. I had been wearing my talisman of carnelian, which protects its owner from the wrath of the Sun God.

⋙ *For a Green Thumb* ⋘

If you've thrown off this life of material gratification, striving in the marketplace, routine, gray weather in the deep, dusty canyons of the city, and have chosen, instead, to loll among the flowers weaving daisy chains in a Vermont commune, then you probably have learned a little something, by now, about farming.

Even in a commune, life isn't all play and sensuality. There's a good deal of effort expended. In fact, instead of total freedom, you have total work. Nothing like starting from scratch to make clothes and food (pick that corn, knead that bread) to make you understand what living used to be all about. And in a commune, that's what living is still all about ("have to build a new tepee today, Anita, the old one's got a hole in the roof").

And then there's the vegetable patch. Women are always in charge of the vegetable patches. You know that big, luscious tomato that's been ripening on the vine and making your mouth water? Do you know anything about those nasty tomato worms that have been watching it ripen, too? I thought not. And the beans. Have you any conception of the amount of time you must spend bent over picking the beans from their stems—one at a time? Hmmm.

Of course, if you're good with trees (climbing them, that

is), you might find happiness in the apple-picking, cherry-picking, and peach-picking department. There are worse ways to spend your days. You could also volunteer as a potato digger.

Whatever you do, if it has to do with farming and growing things, and if you've always had a black thumb, you'd better not "help out" till you've found yourself a jade talisman. Jade, among other things, makes gardens flourish, grass grow, cherry and apple trees give forth sweet, fragrant fruit and, if you wear one, you'll spend your days in peace—tranquilly, successfully, growing things.

⤙ *For Dispelling Sadness* ⤚

When the first warm days come each year, and the air is sweet with an earth smell that's pungent even in the city, penetrating the fumes of overcivilization and touching the heart, it's easy to become susceptible to melancholy. You suddenly want to be out doing things, to be everywhere at once: enjoying a drink in a sidewalk café, or on top of the tallest building breathing in the view, or out strolling in the park feeling the new grass soft and cool on your bare feet, or out on the water moving with the fullness of the air. And usually you can go nowhere, do nothing, just fulfill obligations and carry on life and business as usual. Melancholy settles in then.

You remember when you were a child and were free to play all the summer day long and go out again after dinner. There were swings then, and croquet games, and roaming about in the woods, and playing hide-and-seek and skiprope and jacks. No more freedom now, just memories and melancholy.

Oh, it's not so bad if you can get away and spend a sunny Saturday at the beach, or take a picnic to some mountain fastness where nobody else is. If you can sit under a flowering tree for an hour or two, your spirits will revive. But if you're locked in with your spring fever and your melancholy, you grow quiet, then restless, then frustrated. And there's no one that can help you out of your misery.

If you become desperate, the thing to do is to go to the movies. It's not a cure-all by any means, but a good air-conditioned movie and a bag of popcorn can take you out of yourself and you'll find relief at least for a while. Also, at this precarious time of year, wear a talisman of mother-of-pearl. It lifts spirits, cures feverish ravings of the mind brought on by worry and, when worn in your right ear, improves your memory (so don't wear it in your ear just now. Who needs memories?).

⋖§ *For Pimples* §⋗

With all the delicious healthful foods around today on which to gorge yourself—such as thick, bloody steaks, plump fleshy baked potatoes with six pats of butter oozing around in them, crisp salads of radish and Bermuda onion, iceberg lettuce, and slabs of tomato—you almost have to be some kind of nut to be a junk food freak. Nevertheless, many of us are.

There's nothing quite so satisfying as spending a Sunday afternoon reading a paperback spy book (after finishing *The New York Times*), while consuming a whole giant-sized bag of Frito Cornchips or Tortilla Chips or pretzels or popcorn. Salty, delicious. Right down, the whole bag. Of course, you can't eat dinner, or come Monday the scale will register two pounds more than Sunday.

And then there are French-fried onion rings. Very, very difficult to find a decent French-fried onion ring, you know. If you're a connoisseur, you make the rounds of all the local hot-dog stands and other informal eateries till you find what you're after: light, airy, fluffy rings with the batter browned to just the right crispiness. If the chef changes jobs, you track him down.

Ice cream can be a problem. If you don't have a Howard Johnson's or a Schrafft's, or a special homemade ice cream parlor (though here we may be leaving the proper realm of junk food) you might have to put up with something utterly tasteless like Borden's. What a shame. It's possible, however, to find satisfaction with Cool 'n' Creamy.

Whatever delicacies are your private thing, the net result of eating them is a faceful of pimples. Even in your late twenties, pimples [sob] still strike. The talisman stone for you to wear, then, is marvelous coral, that soft, Campbell's-tomato-soup-colored jewel that guarantees a skin free of those nasty little red pustules. (A side benefit from coral is that it keeps you safe from drowning when you're in the water.)

✑§ *For High Fever* ဇ✒

If you tried to get out of bed this morning, but found yourself unable to stir up enough energy even to raise your head from the pillow, you'd better think, right away, about whom you might have insulted recently. When your body goes so limp with fatigue that not even a fire in your bedroom could hurry you from your horizontal recline, you've either got mononucleosis or are the victim of an attack of witchcraft.

When you're involved in witchcraft, the chances of having it worked against you are the same as the chances of your working it against someone else. And one of the favorite enchantments that witches indulge in (it doesn't kill the victim, only incapacitates him) is the one that drains away bodily strength.

Other symptoms may accompany your total languor, if the witch is proficient. Making the subject throw up is a favorite torture extra. And I don't mean the once or twice rush-to-the-bathroom variety of nausea; I mean the marathon kind where you're almost better off camped by the toilet (not so hard on weakened legs). Another torture is the roaring headache, akin to the migraine. This is especially effective with victims who aren't usually subject to migraine, as the pain is unfamiliar and therefore doubly excruciating and fear-making.

A truly superior witch may add to your complete exhaustion, nausea, and headache a really roaring fever. The doctor won't be able to comprehend why you have it, and icepacks won't help much in breaking it. You'll just simply have this fever and it will worsen and worsen till you're possessed. You'll start hallucinating devils with horns and monsters with gray-green faces. If you have a ruby talisman, hold it in your hand. In a few hours, the fever will break, your nausea will recede, your headache will stop throbbing, and your strength will return. Without the ruby it's possible for the delirium to continue through the day. If I were you, I certainly wouldn't get myself involved with witchcraft without having at least a small ruby near at hand for protection against such a day.

Appendix: Herb Shops

It's not easy to come across stores around the country that sell esoteric herbs, but in New York there are several. If you live in the city, the place to go for your exotic ingredients is Kiehl Pharmacy, Inc., at 13th Street and Third Avenue. On hand are over two thousand herbs, and the supply is growing (the owner spends two or three months every year traveling about the world collecting new herbs and replenishing depleted stocks). But, sadness, Kiehl's won't ship —too much paperwork involved, they say.

Thankfully, this is not the case with Goodman Pharmacy, 1634 Second Avenue, New York, N.Y. 10028, which does a thriving business cross-country. They say they're happy to ship if the order is three dollars or more. What you should do is write to them and list the herbs you want (and how much of each), and ask if they can get them for you. They'll respond accordingly. Goodman's has an enormous stock of esoteric herbs, too—everything from assafoetida to worm-wood, including nettle.

If Goodman doesn't have it, write to Aphrodisia, 28 Carmine Street, New York, N.Y. 10014. Their catalogue includes such necessities as ginseng, musk, mastic gum, verbena root, and yarrow. It also states, "If you are interested in something not listed here, please ask about it . . . Anything that we don't have in stock, we will do our best to locate for you." They're new, so they're trying harder.

If you feel that you would like to deal with the oldest pharmacy in New York, however, write to the apothecary, Caswell-Massey Co., Ltd., 518 Lexington Avenue, New York, N.Y. 10017. They've been around since 1752. While they don't ordinarily stock esoteric herbs, they say they'll be delighted to try to get whatever it is you ask for. They're good, willing, reliable people (the secret to their longevity).

Now, on the matter of acquiring adder's tongues, henbane, blood of doves, and other oddities, I can only offer you the following advice. If you live near Mexico, you're in luck. These ingredients are common south of the border. If you live in New York, you may also be in luck. There is a little botánica called Arte Espiritual on 104th Street between Park and Lexington Avenues. It is run by an old adept named Justo, who may be the only man in New York from whom you can purchase such items. He is very, very loath, however, to acknowledge that he knows anything at all about them. It would behoove you, therefore, to make friends with Justo, via several visits to purchase his goods (fresh herbs, etc.) so that when you spring adder's tongues on him, or hen's blood, he won't have an attack. Again, as with all else in magic, wit and perseverance are required.

I'm afraid that between the East Coast and the West there is a great hinterland that (except in Chicago and parts of the South) is nearly devoid of unusual magical additives. There is only one way, then, to gather your ingredients, and that is ingeniously. Asking about (a hushed voice helps) may produce some specific person to see, but chances are you'll probably have to catch your own chicken or buy a pheasant at a wild-game butcher's in the end.

But the herbs are easy (though you're going to have trouble with henbane, as the Food and Drug Administration has outlawed it). Vervain, hellebore, sulfur, salep, aloes wood, wormwood, valerian, jasmine, coriander, white pepper, pine nuts, mandrake, rue, hemlock, and the dozens of other herbs mentioned in this book are readily available through the sources I've listed.

Index